DRAWING WILD ANIMALS

BY JOYCE HAYNES

Weekly Reader Books
MIDDLETOWN, CONNECTICUT

Publishing, Executive, and Editorial Offices:
Weekly Reader Books
Field Publications
Middletown, CT 06457

Introduction

Wild animals of all shapes and sizes live all over the world. This book is designed to teach you how to draw wild animals by looking at each one as a series of shapes. By combining basic shapes, you will be able to draw wild animals that range from the jawless anteater to the toothy alligator.

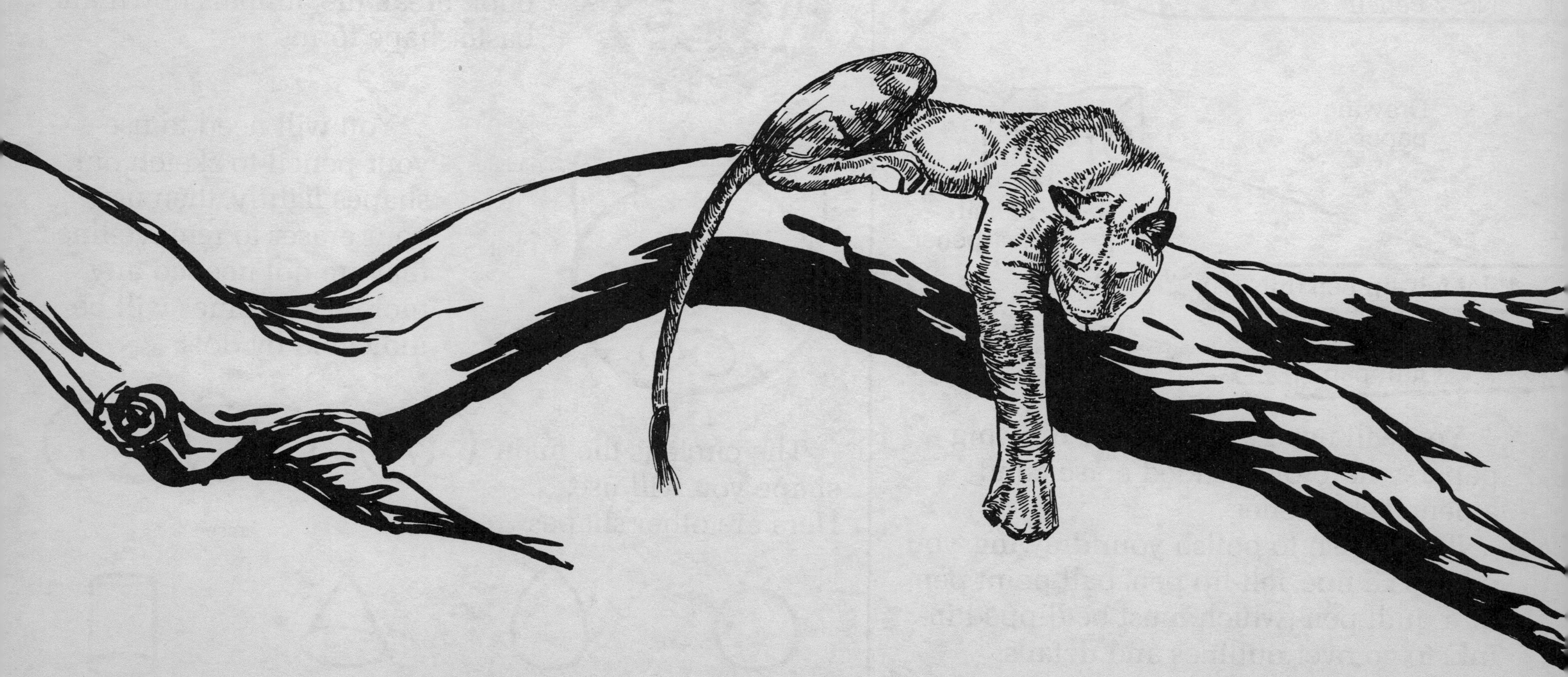

Materials

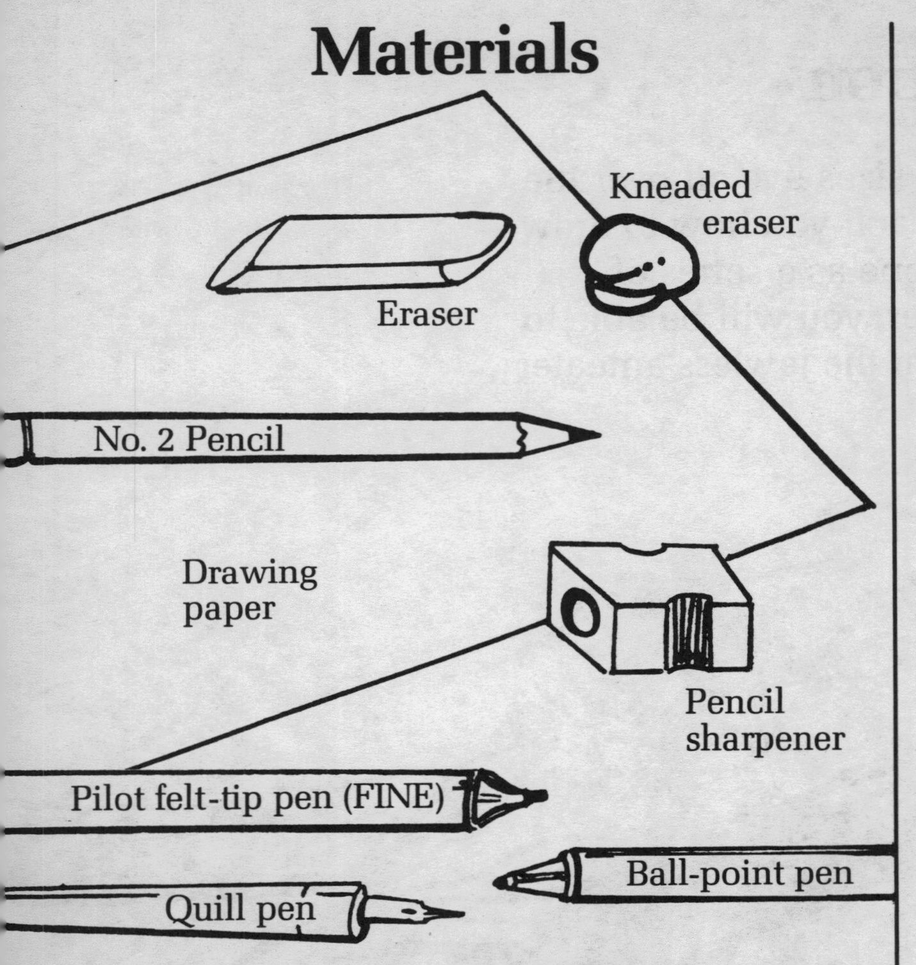

You will need a soft pencil, drawing paper, a hard or kneaded eraser, and a pencil sharpener.

If you wish to polish your drawing, you can use a fine, felt-tip pen, ball-point pen, or a quill pen (which must be dipped in ink) to go over outlines and details.

Drawing wild animals can be lots of fun and easy too! Just keep these hints in mind. . . .

When you are drawing an animal, consider it as a combination of shapes. The lessons in this book break the animals down into basic shape forms.

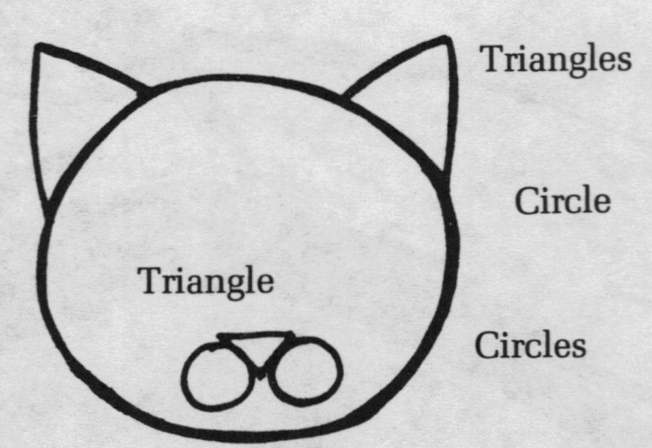

You will need to use your pencil to sketch out shapes *lightly*, then use your eraser to remove lines that are not needed any more. These lines will be indicated by dots.

The circle is the main shape you will use. Here are other shapes:

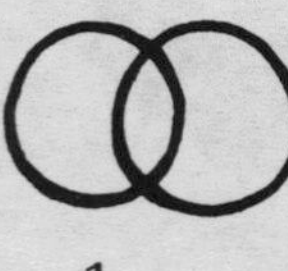

circle

oval (egg shape)

cone

cylinder

Drawing Animal Fur

Thick, Stringy Hair

1 The llama has thick, stringy fur. Draw the fur with few lines, making hair curve.

2 To make fur appear thicker and shadowed, draw with quick, downward strokes (curved and overlapping lines). The more lines you draw, the darker the fur will appear.

3 To show shadows, completely color in those areas.

4 Perhaps the wind is blowing a long-haired animal's fur. Indicate this by drawing long strokes that curve left or right, in whatever direction the wind is blowing. Overlap lines.

1 The bighorn sheep has short fur. When drawing short fur, make quick, short strokes. The farther apart the strokes, the lighter the fur will appear. Tight, overlapping strokes darken fur.

Light **DARK**

2 When drawing the outline of an animal, draw rough, uneven lines to indicate fur.

3 Shadows give pictures contrast and make them stand out.

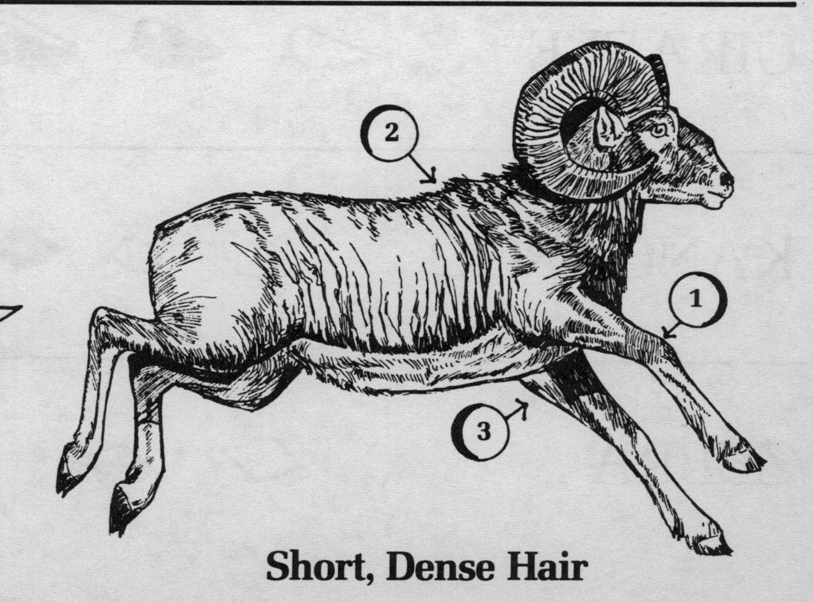

Short, Dense Hair

Animal Eyes

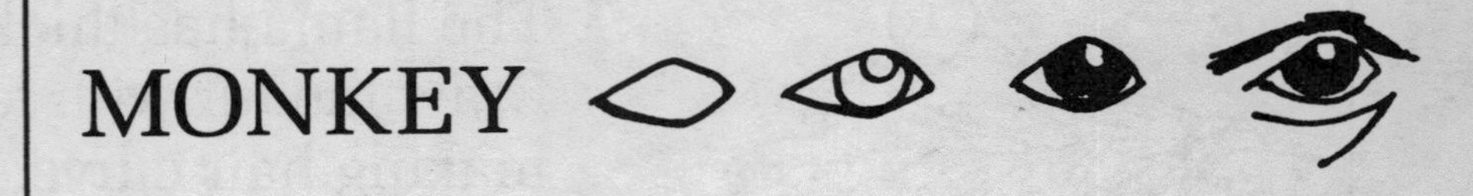

These are examples of different animals' eyes. You may wish to refer to this page when you have started drawing.

LION

MONKEY

KOALA

ELEPHANT

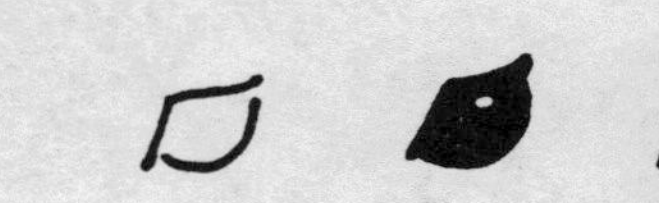

RHINOCEROS

GIRAFFE

OSTRICH

KANGAROO

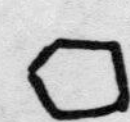

CAMEL

ZEBRA

HIPPOPOTAMUS

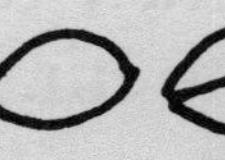

Lion

Lions are native to Africa. They live in prides of 15 or more lions and like to relax on tree limbs, although they are not very good climbers.

Step 1

To draw a lion, start with three oval shapes placed as shown. The largest oval will be for the head.

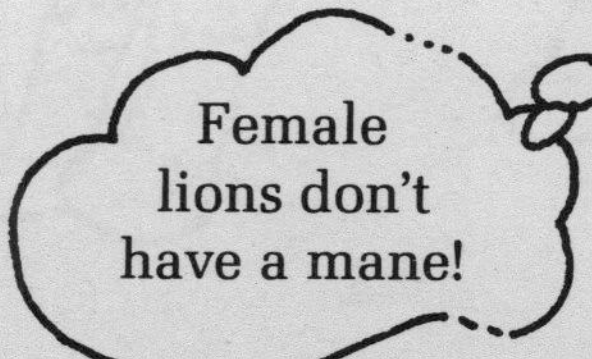

Step 2

Draw small circles to indicate positions of the knees and paws. Draw an oval in the center of the head shape. Draw a cross in this oval. Draw the back outline. Erase where the dotted lines indicate.

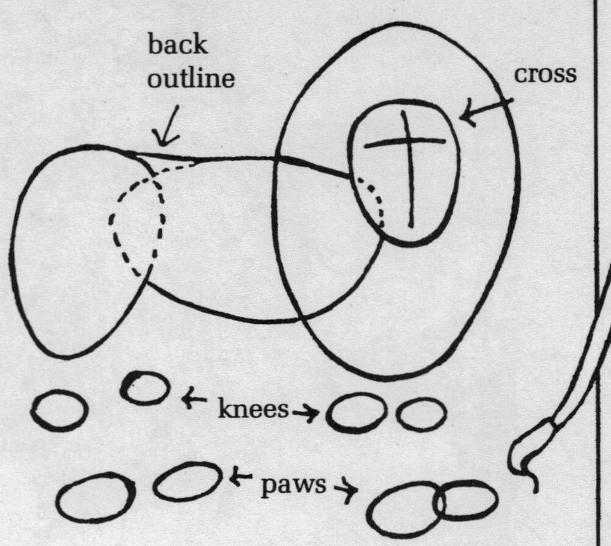

Step 3

Add the tail and connect the small circles to form legs. Draw eyes left and right of the cross-lines intersection. The nose is a triangle shape centered at the base of the cross. Draw a mouth and ears.

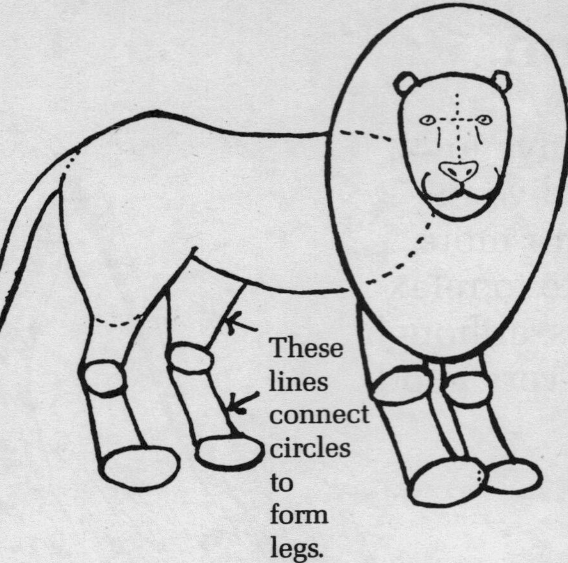

Step 4

Draw ragged lines for hair on the mane and the chin. Erase where the dotted lines indicate.

Step 5

Add whiskers and claws. Sketch hair lines on mane (long lines) and body (short lines). Darker areas make contrasting shadows.

Elephant

The elephant's thick skin acts as insulation to maintain an even temperature in its body. This large animal also flaps its ears to fan itself. Elephants are found in Asia and Africa.

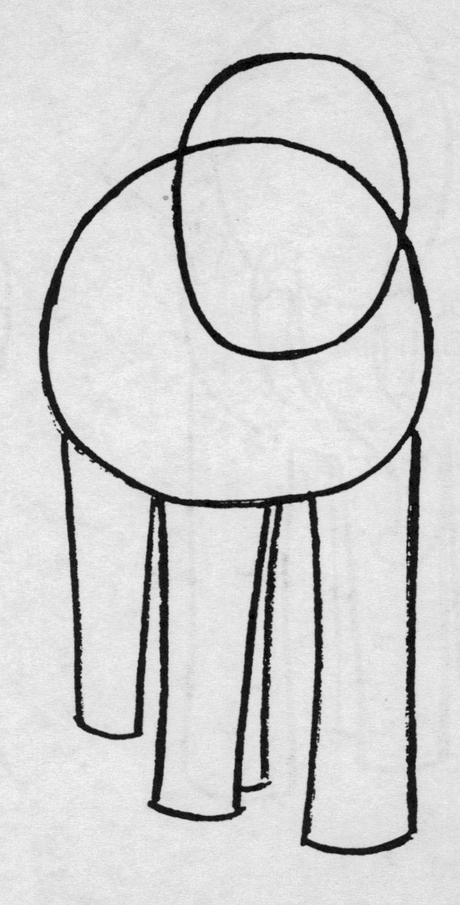

Step 1

To draw an elephant, start with a large circle for the body shape and an oval for the head (position as shown). For the legs, draw cylinder shapes.

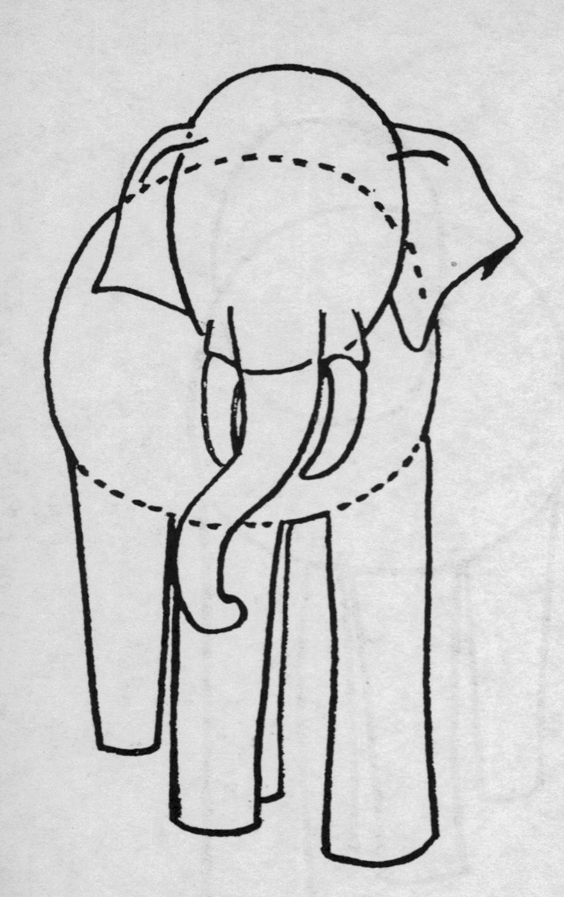

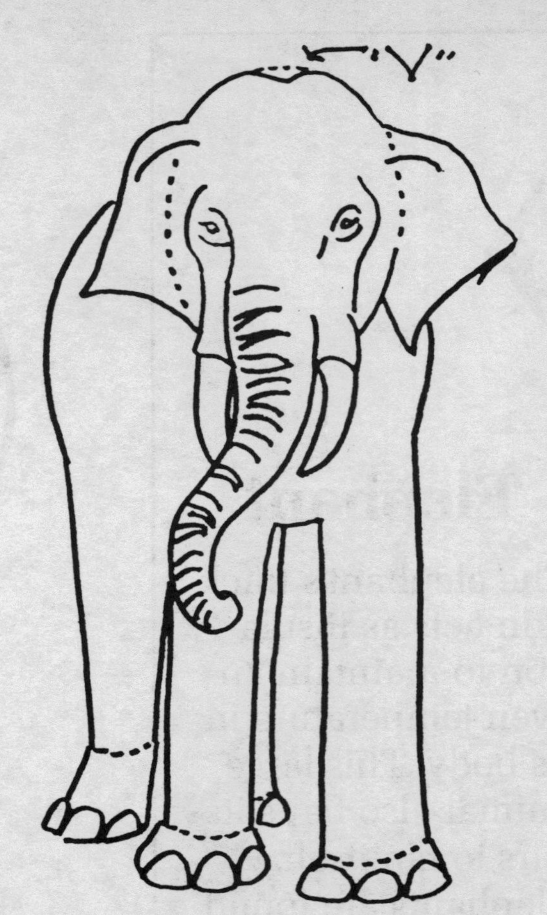

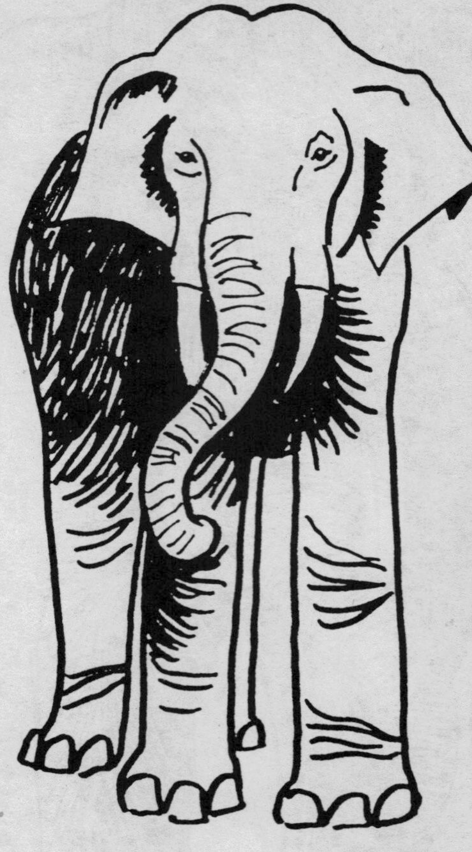

We elephants have very tough, wrinkled skin. So draw lots of wrinkles on me!

Step 2

Add ears, tusks, and a trunk. Erase where the dotted lines indicate.

Step 3

Make a *V* line on top of the head. Add eyes. Then draw lines from the tusks around and past the eyes. Draw wrinkle lines on trunk. Add toes.

Step 4

Draw wrinkle lines on legs (long, downward strokes). Draw shadows (solid areas and overlapping strokes).

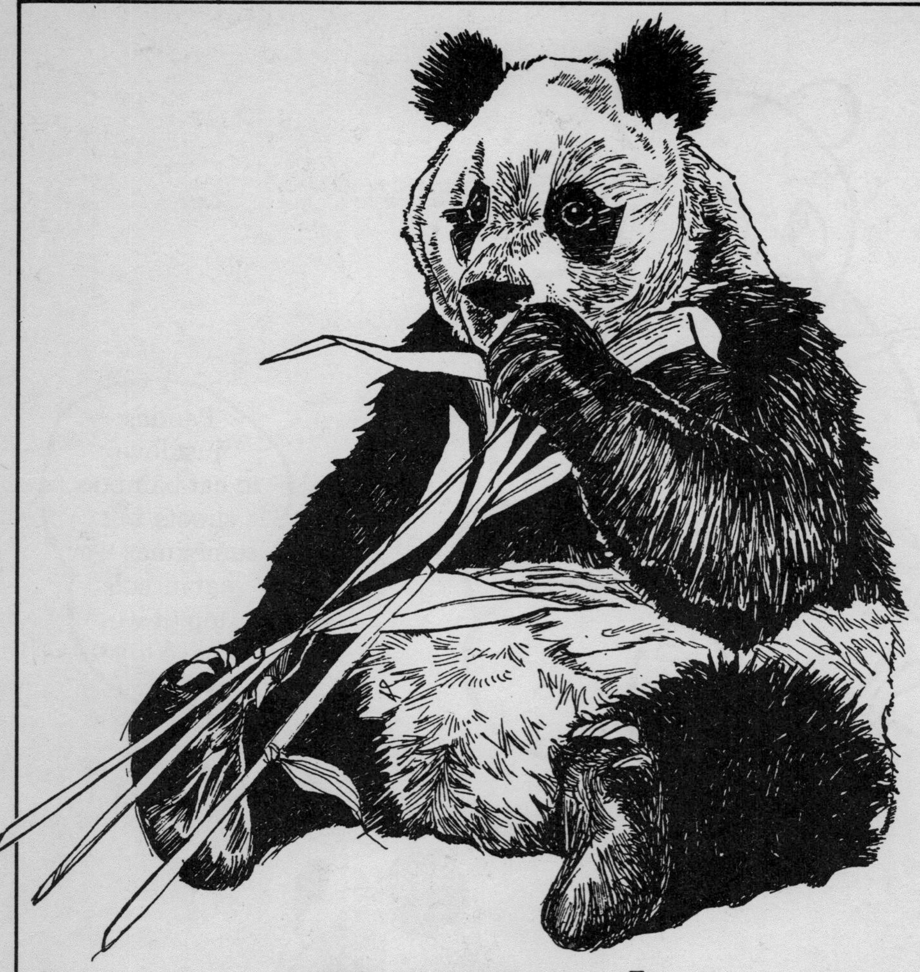

Giant Panda

The giant panda is one of the best known and most popular mammals today. This large bear eats only bamboo shoots and is found in China and on the Chinese-Tibetan border.

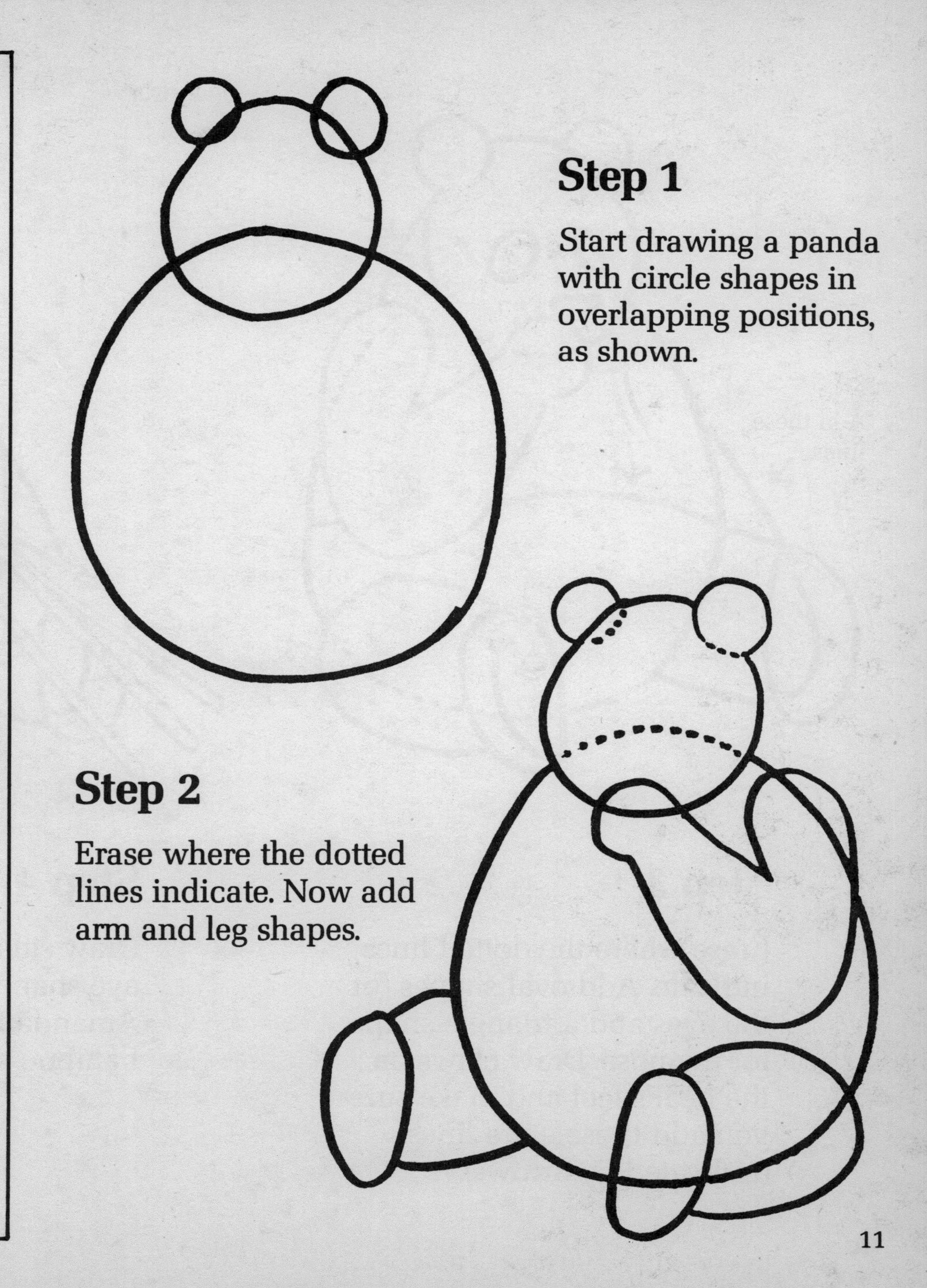

Step 1

Start drawing a panda with circle shapes in overlapping positions, as shown.

Step 2

Erase where the dotted lines indicate. Now add arm and leg shapes.

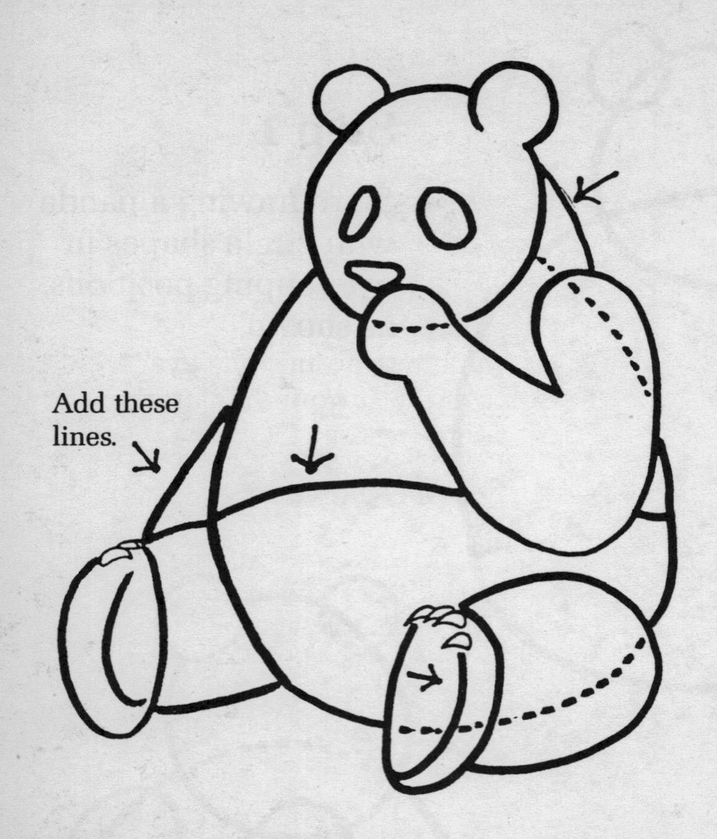

Step 3

Erase where the dotted lines indicate. Add oval shapes for the eyes and a triangle shape for the nose. Draw claws on the bear's feet and make sure you add those extra lines (indicated by arrows).

Step 4

Draw small circles in the oval eye shapes. Then add Amanda Panda's favorite bamboo shoots.

Pandas just love to eat bamboo shoots, but sometimes we eat insects too (if we have to)!

Step 5

Shade the dark eye patches (see helpful hint).
At this point, you may want to begin shading and outlining your drawing with a pen or you may prefer to continue with pencil. Shade the nose.

• Helpful Hint •

1.  2.  3. 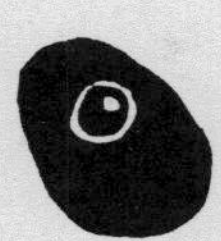

Shading the Eye

1. Color in the eyeball.
2. Draw a circle around the eyeball.
3. Color in the surrounding area.

Step 6

Draw hair lines with downward, medium strokes, overlapping so that the fur appears darker. (See "Drawing Animal Fur," page 5.) Draw a few lines on the face and belly.

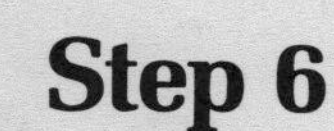

Zebra

Zebras live in Africa in groups of 5 to 15. They feed on wild grasses.

Step 1

Circle shapes, positioned as shown above, will start your drawing of a zebra.

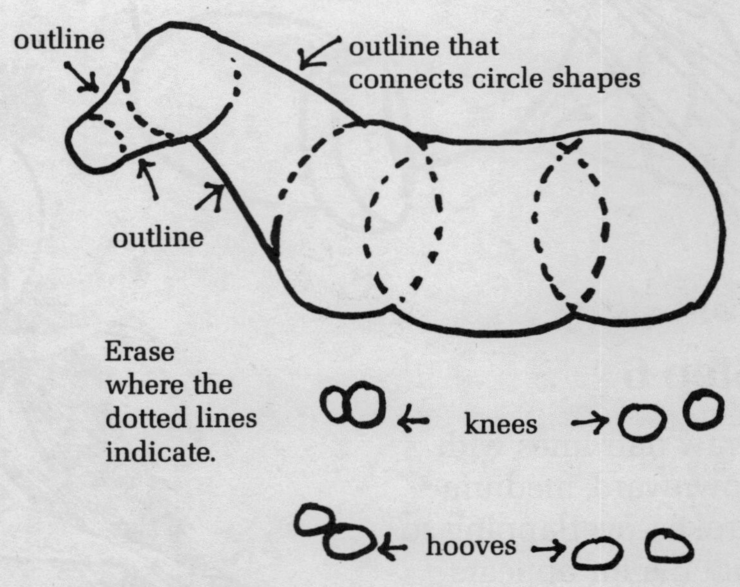

Step 2

Draw an outline that connects the circles, then draw small circles to indicate the knees and hooves.

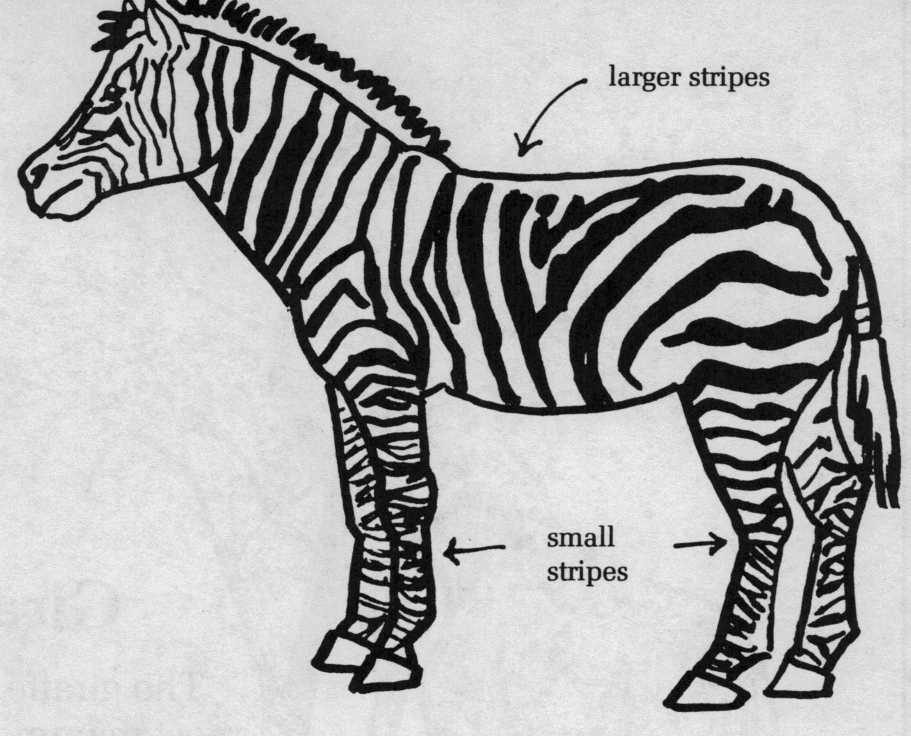

Step 3

Draw legs by connecting the knee and hoof circles. Then add a mane and tail and put in ears, a nose, a mouth, and eyes.

The eye is like an almond in shape!

eye

almond shape

Step 4

Straighten hoof lines so they appear sharp rather than rounded. Add stripes.

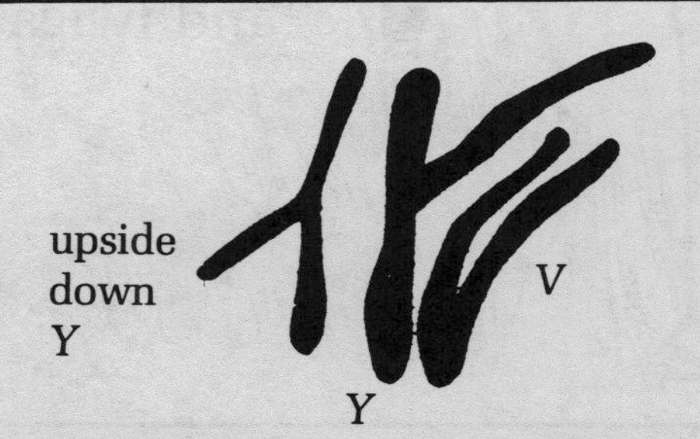

• Helpful Hint •

Many stripes are in a *Y* or *V* shape. Vary size by making smaller stripes on legs and face.

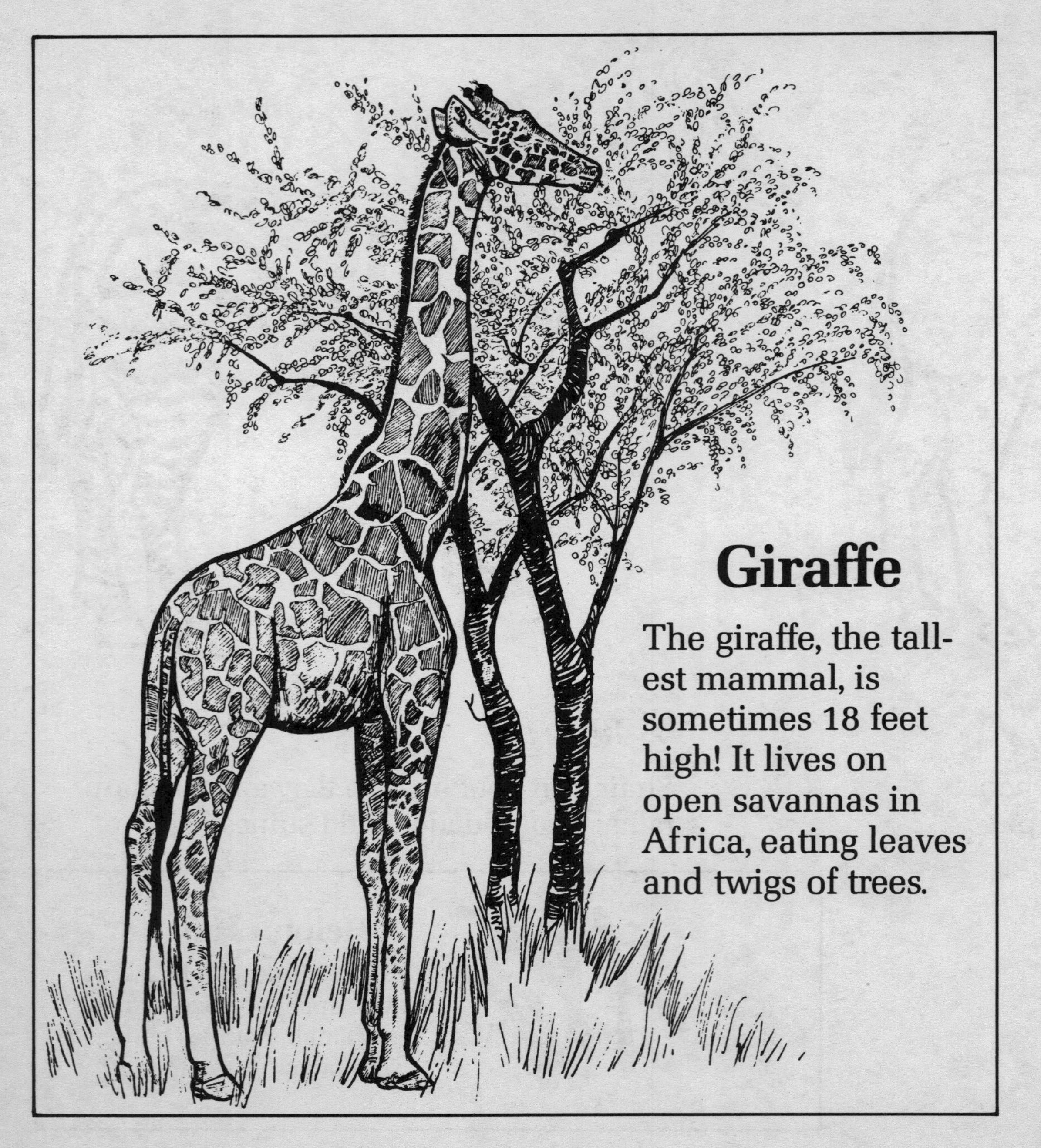

Giraffe

The giraffe, the tallest mammal, is sometimes 18 feet high! It lives on open savannas in Africa, eating leaves and twigs of trees.

Step 1

Start with circle shapes positioned as shown to draw a giraffe.

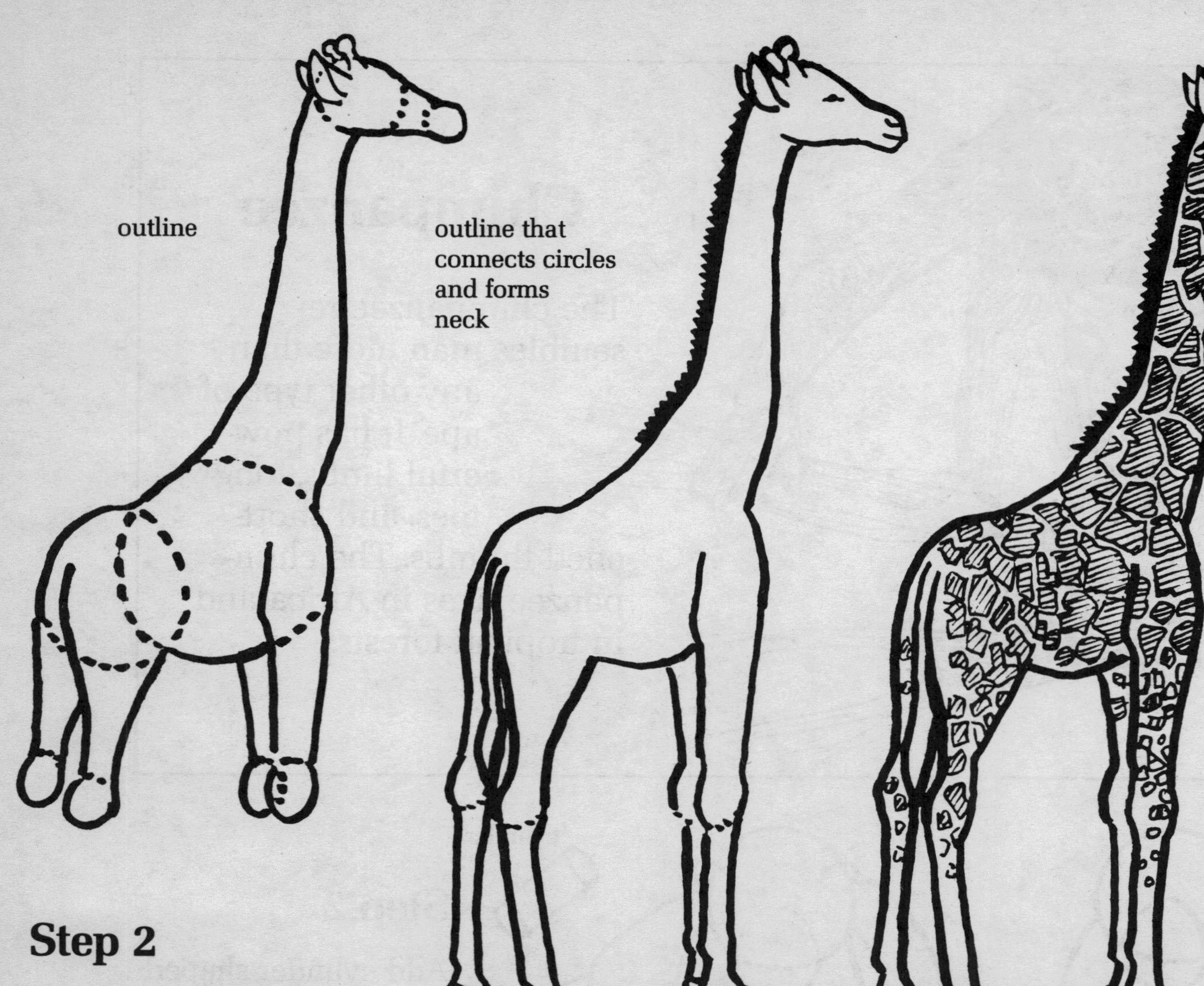

Giraffe's skin pattern has smaller markings on face and legs!

Step 2

Connect the circles with an outline, forming neck and legs. Draw the ears and horns. Erase where the dotted lines indicate.

Step 3

Draw eyes, nose, mouth, mane, and tail. Add lower legs and hooves.

Step 4

Draw the skin pattern (see helpful hint).

Use long strokes that cover the area, and space lines so they don't overlap.

• Helpful Hint •

When drawing a giraffe's skin pattern, draw square-type shapes that almost fit together like puzzle pieces.

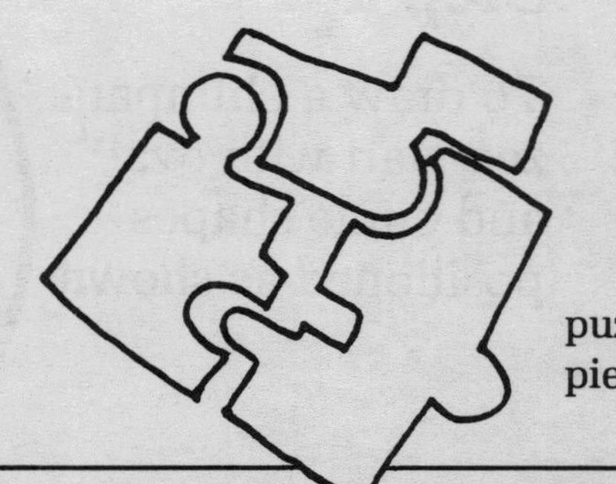

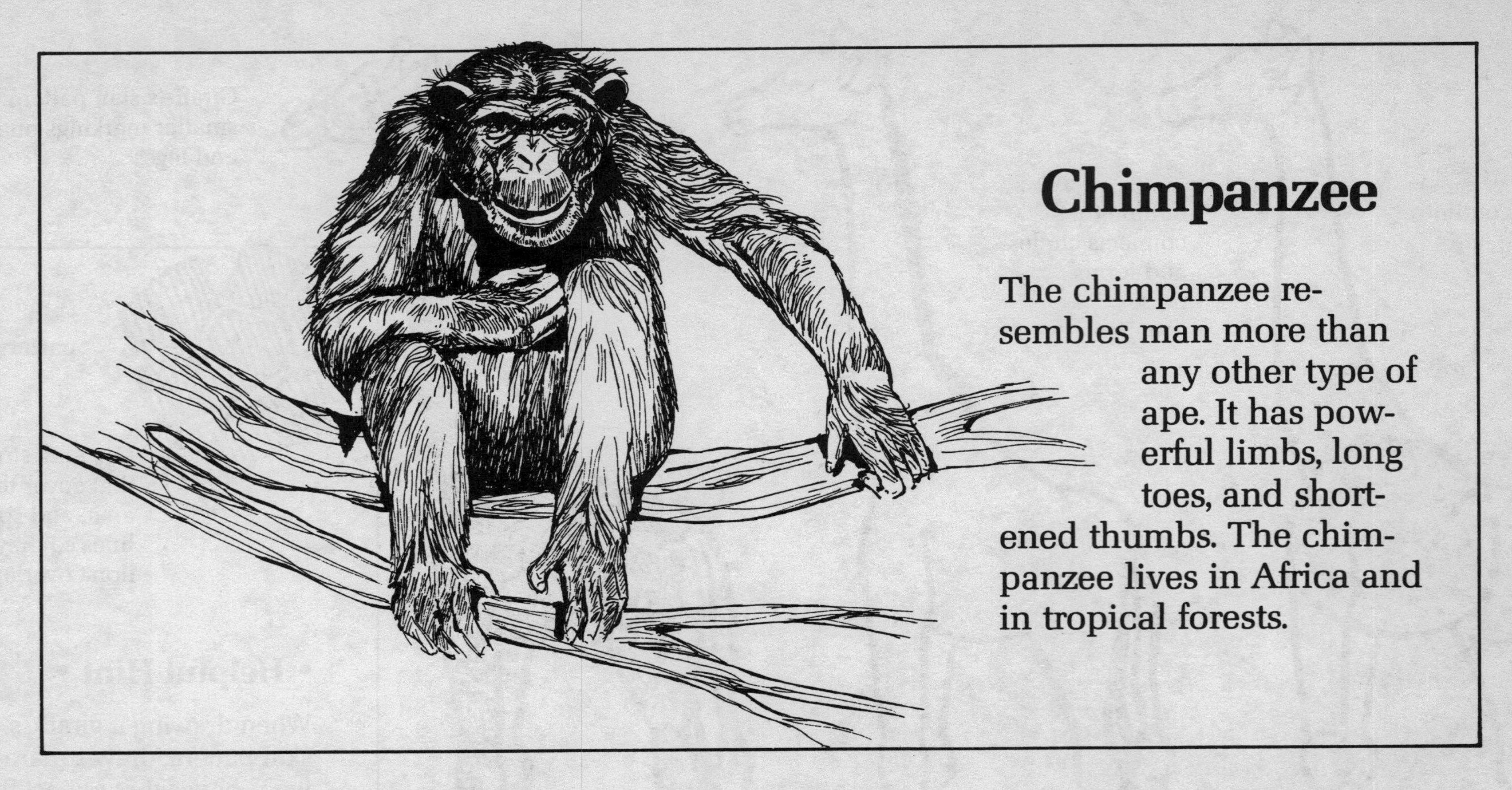

Chimpanzee

The chimpanzee resembles man more than any other type of ape. It has powerful limbs, long toes, and shortened thumbs. The chimpanzee lives in Africa and in tropical forests.

Step 1

To draw a chimpanzee, start with oval and circle shapes positioned as shown.

Step 2

Add cylinder-shaped ears, arms, and hands. Erase where the dotted lines indicate.

Step 3

Draw fingers on the hands. Legs also are cylinder-shaped and the feet look like hands. Be sure to draw the extra line by the leg (see arrow).

Step 4

Draw eyebrows (shaped like a flat *M*) on the face. Add the eyes, a mouth, and a nose. Remember to draw wrinkles under chimp's eyes.

Step 5

For finishing touches, add tree limbs, hair on the body, and shadows. Draw the shadows on the ears, under chimp's chin, legs, and hands. Add wrinkles on its mouth.

Dromedary

A one-humped camel that lives in the Sahara desert, the dromedary is capable of surviving long periods of time without water. When water is available, the camel can hold up to 15 gallons!

Step 1

To draw a dromedary, start with oval and circle shapes positioned as shown.

Step 2

Add a line that outlines and connects the circles. Erase where the dotted lines indicate. Add a tail, ears, eyes, a nose, and a mouth.

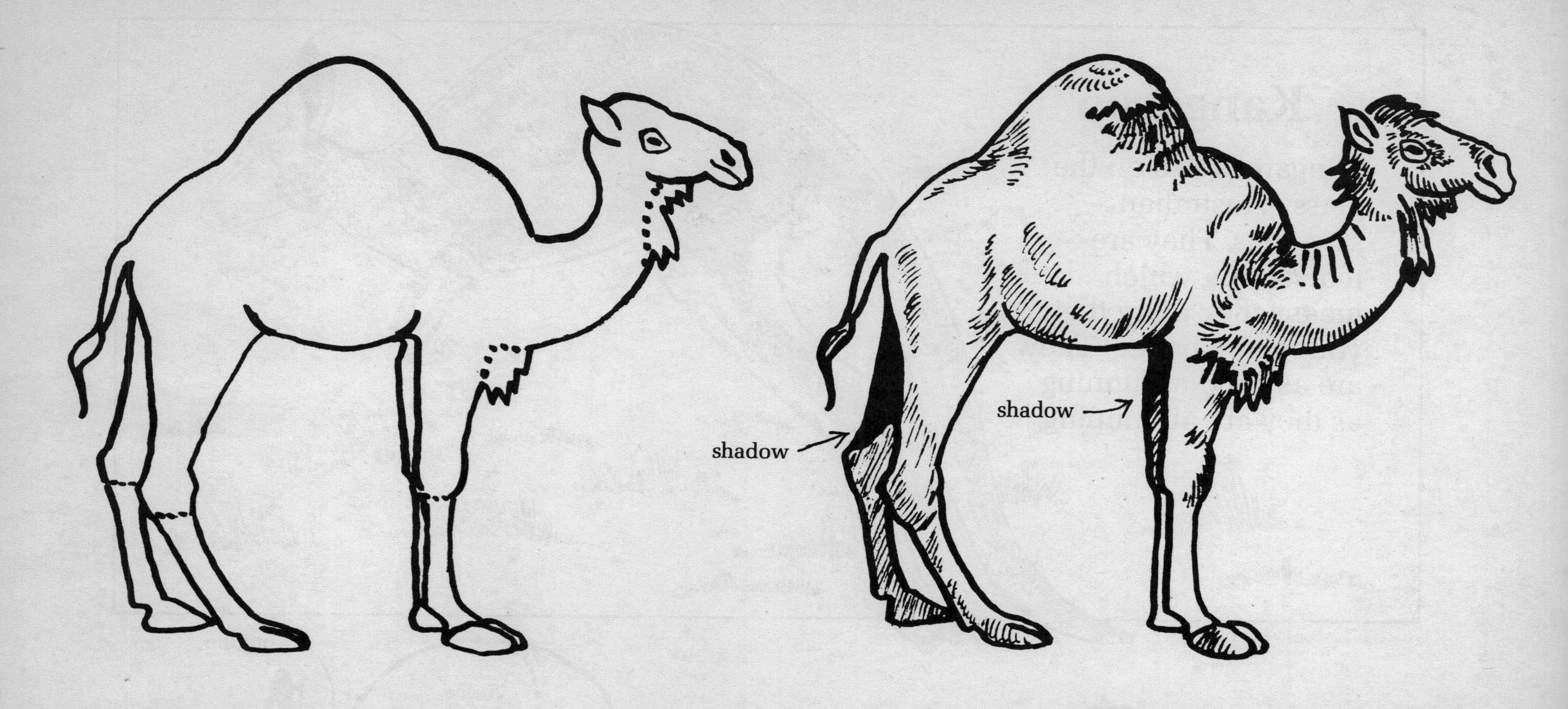

Step 3

Draw lower legs and feet (see detail below). Add hair lines where arrows indicate and a light circle around the eye.

toes

joint

Step 4

Shade in shadows, draw hair lines, and be sure to add short hair lines surrounding the light circle around the eye.

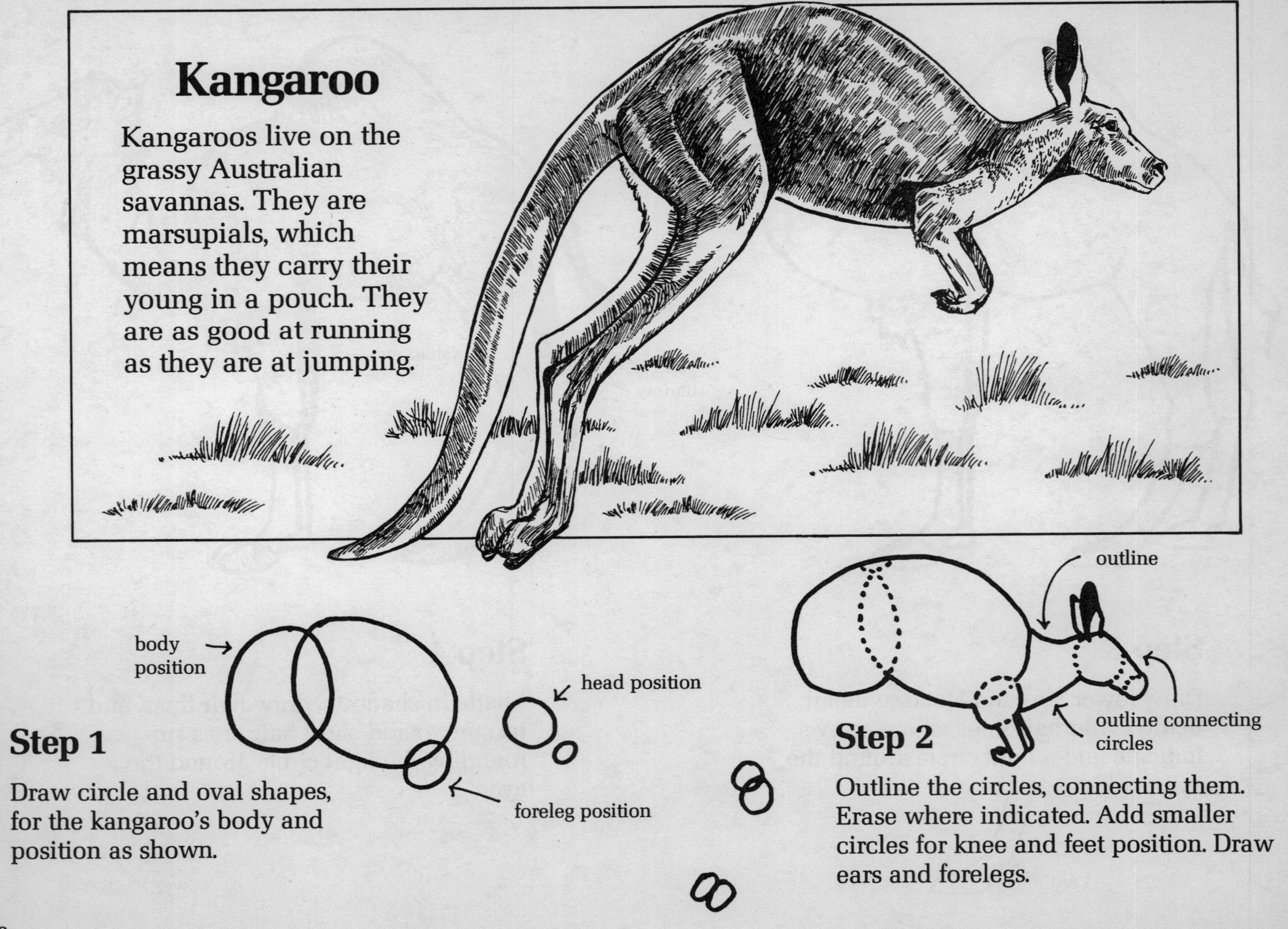

Kangaroo

Kangaroos live on the grassy Australian savannas. They are marsupials, which means they carry their young in a pouch. They are as good at running as they are at jumping.

Step 1

Draw circle and oval shapes, for the kangaroo's body and position as shown.

Step 2

Outline the circles, connecting them. Erase where indicated. Add smaller circles for knee and feet position. Draw ears and forelegs.

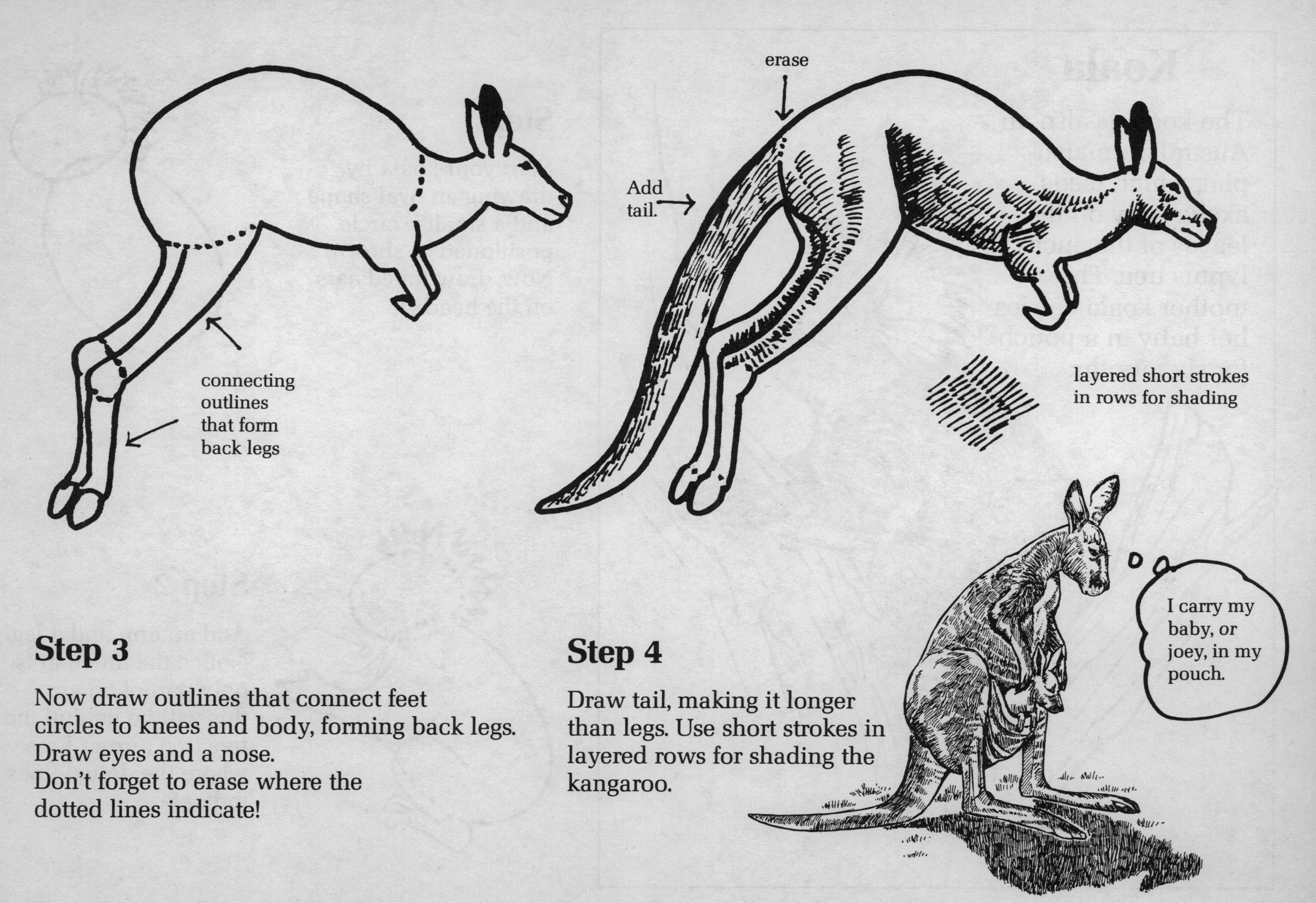

Step 3

Now draw outlines that connect feet
circles to knees and body, forming back legs.
Draw eyes and a nose.
Don't forget to erase where the
dotted lines indicate!

Step 4

Draw tail, making it longer
than legs. Use short strokes in
layered rows for shading the
kangaroo.

Koala

The koala is also an Australian marsupial, which feeds exclusively on the leaves of the eucalyptus tree. The mother koala carries her baby in a pouch for six months.

Step 1

Start your koala by drawing an oval shape and a smaller circle, positioned as shown. Now, draw tufted ears on the head.

Step 2

Add an arm and a leg. Notice the line that is only part of an arm—this will be behind the tree (see arrow). Erase where the dotted lines indicate.

Step 3

Add a nose and a mouth. Draw a small eye with a lightly drawn circle around it.

Step 4

Draw the tree. Shade the koala by using small strokes that curve as body outlines curve (see detail above).

Rhinoceros

The rhinoceros lives in African savannas or dense, thorny bush country. Rhinos use their lips to break and tear at twigs and leaves.

Step 1

The head and body positions of a rhinoceros are modified cylinder shapes. Draw them so they overlap.

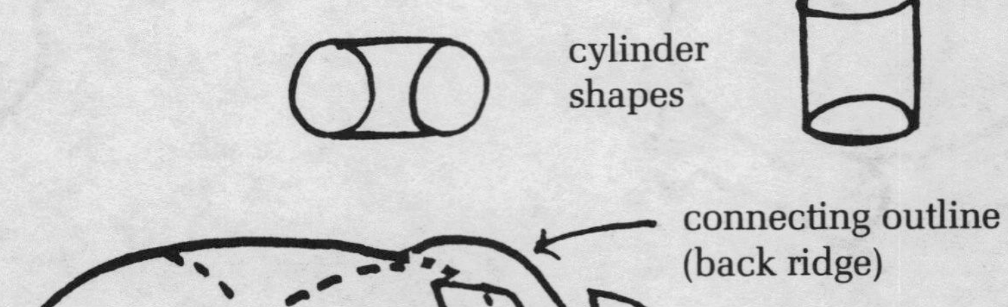

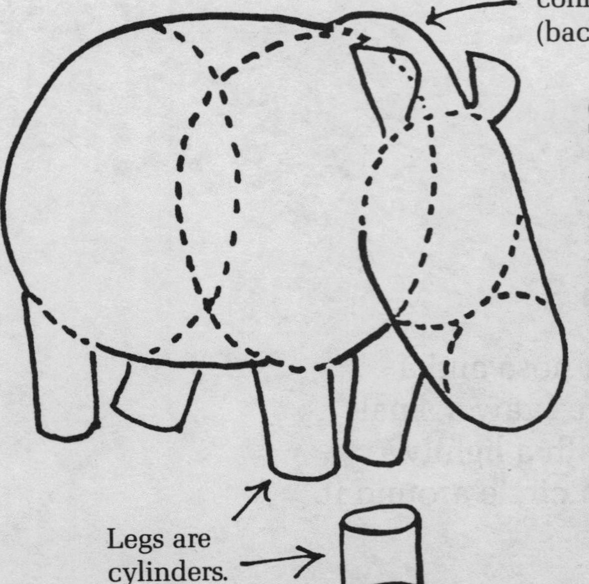

Step 2

Erase where the dotted lines indicate. Draw ears and add legs (cylinder shapes). Draw outline connecting the head to the body. Put a slight lump on it—the back ridge.

Don't forget to erase where the dotted lines indicate!

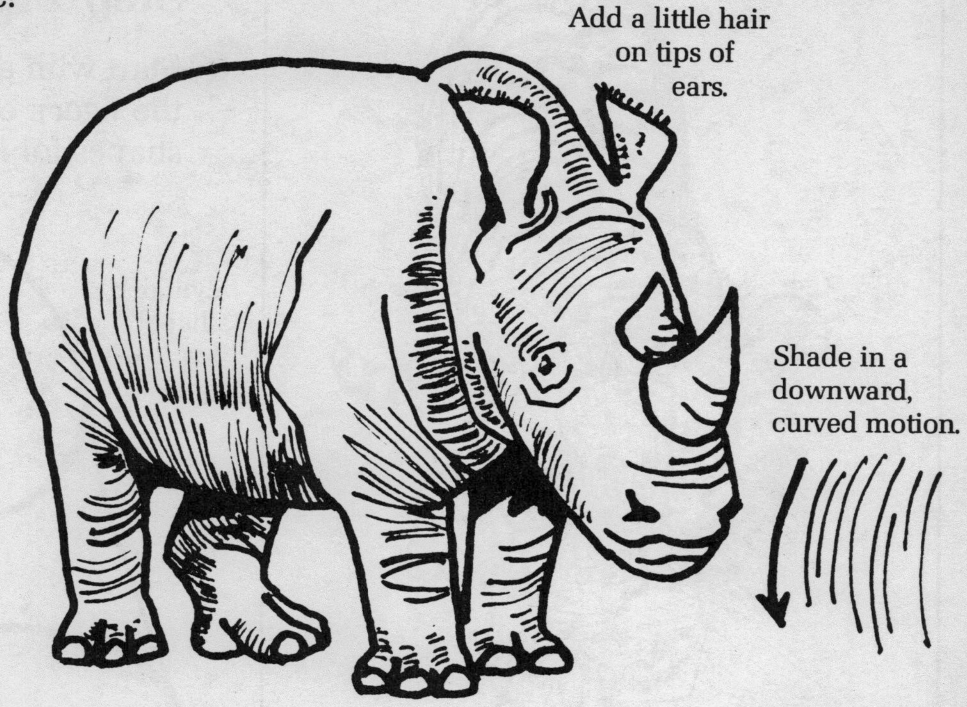

Step 3

Add three toes with large toenails to the bottoms of the legs. Add cone-shaped horns, one smaller than the other. Put in nostrils, mouth, eyes, and wrinkles around the eyes.

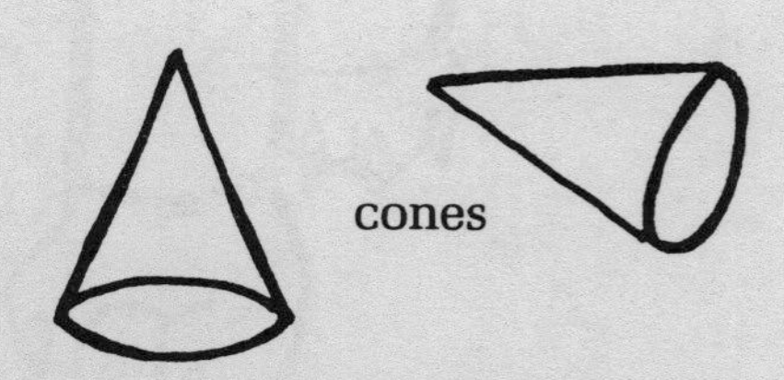

Step 4

When shading the rhino, which has very tough, leathery skin, draw long and short lines side by side in a curved motion. Fill in shadowed areas.

Tiger

The tiger is the largest carnivore (meat eater) and cat. These animals prefer to roam in thick forests or jungles.

Step 1

Start with a large cylinder for the tiger's body. Use cylinder shapes for legs too.

Step 2

Draw a cross in the head circle. Add ears, tail, and paws.

Step 3

Draw eyes on either side of the cross intersection. Place a triangular-shaped nose at the end of the cross, and draw cheeks, chin hair, and long whiskers!

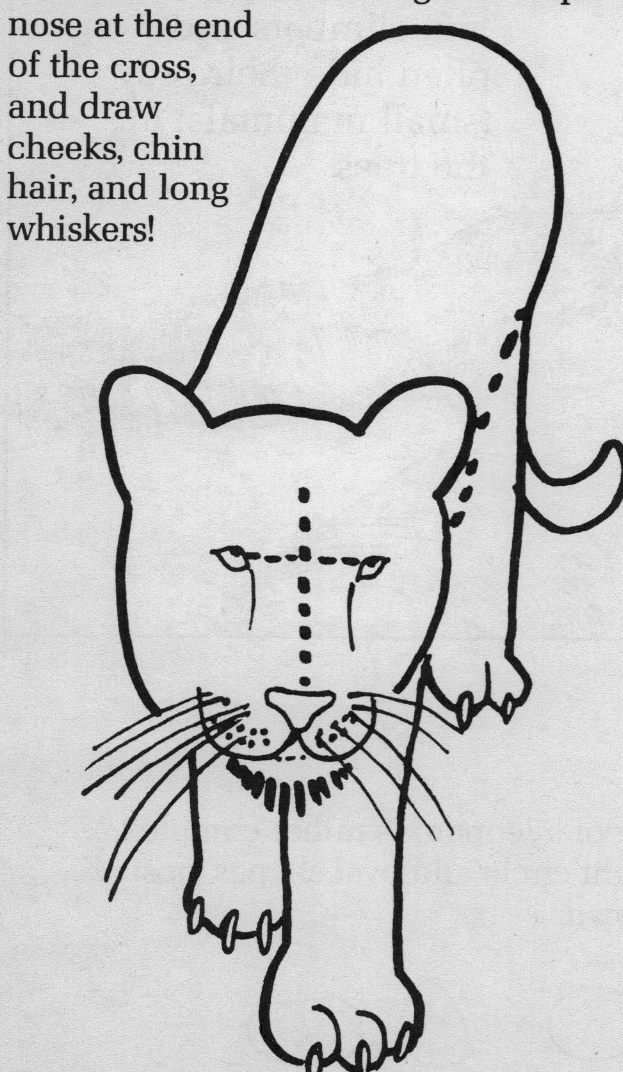

Step 4

Add shading and stripes.

• Helpful Hint •

When drawing stripes, draw some of them like variations of the letter *V*.

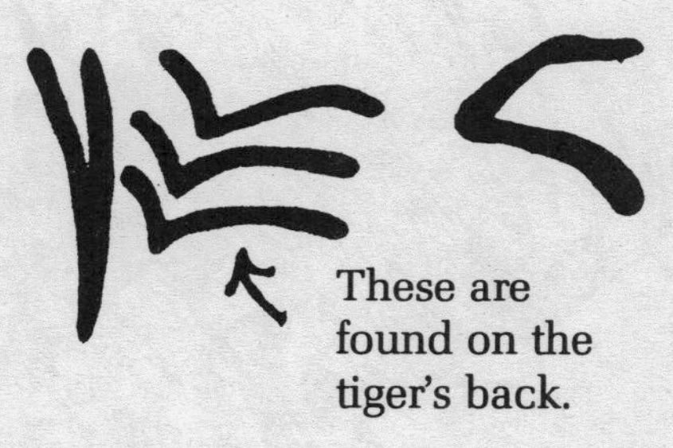

Shade the face with short lines around the nose and medium strokes around the face. Draw hair in the ears also.

Leopard

Leopards are excellent climbers and often hide their prey (small mammals) in the trees.

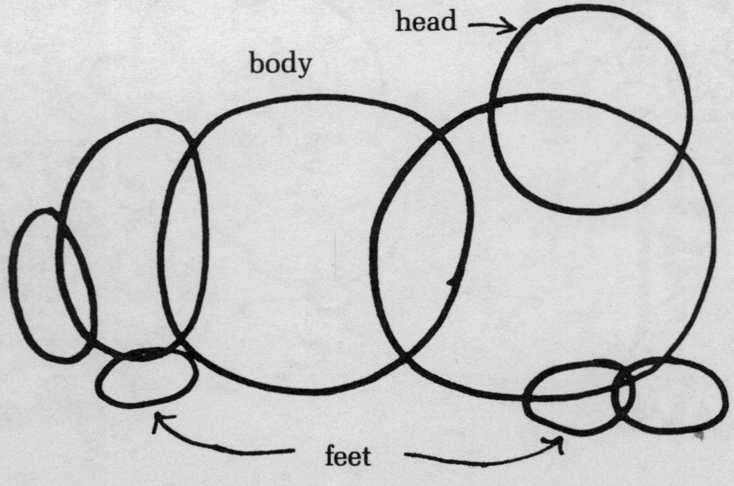

Step 1

This drawing of a leopard is rather complex. Start with eight circle and oval shapes, positioned as shown.

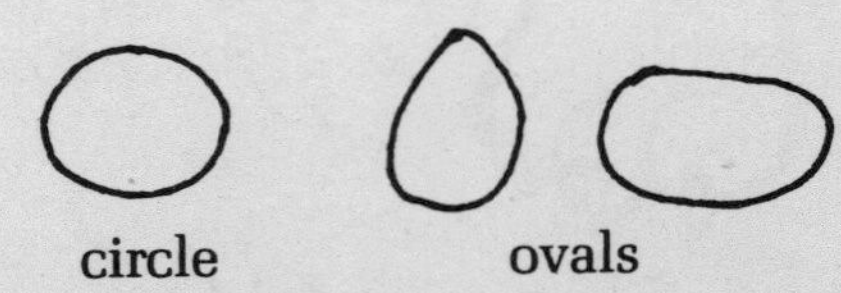

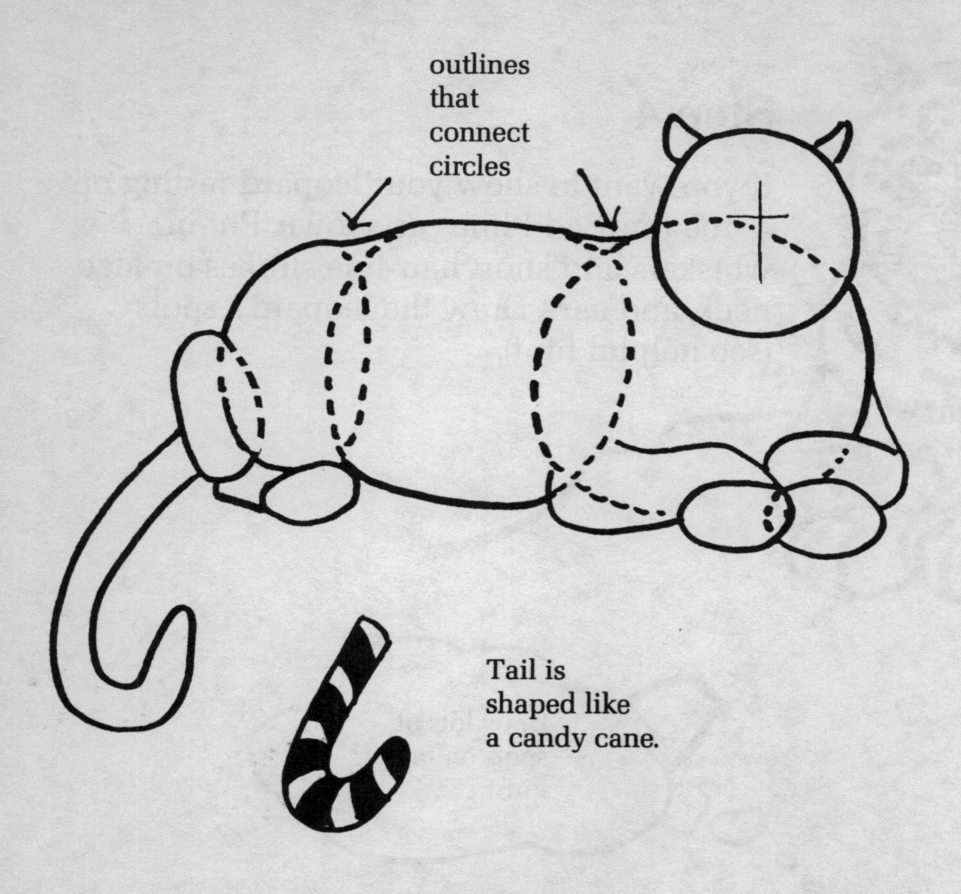

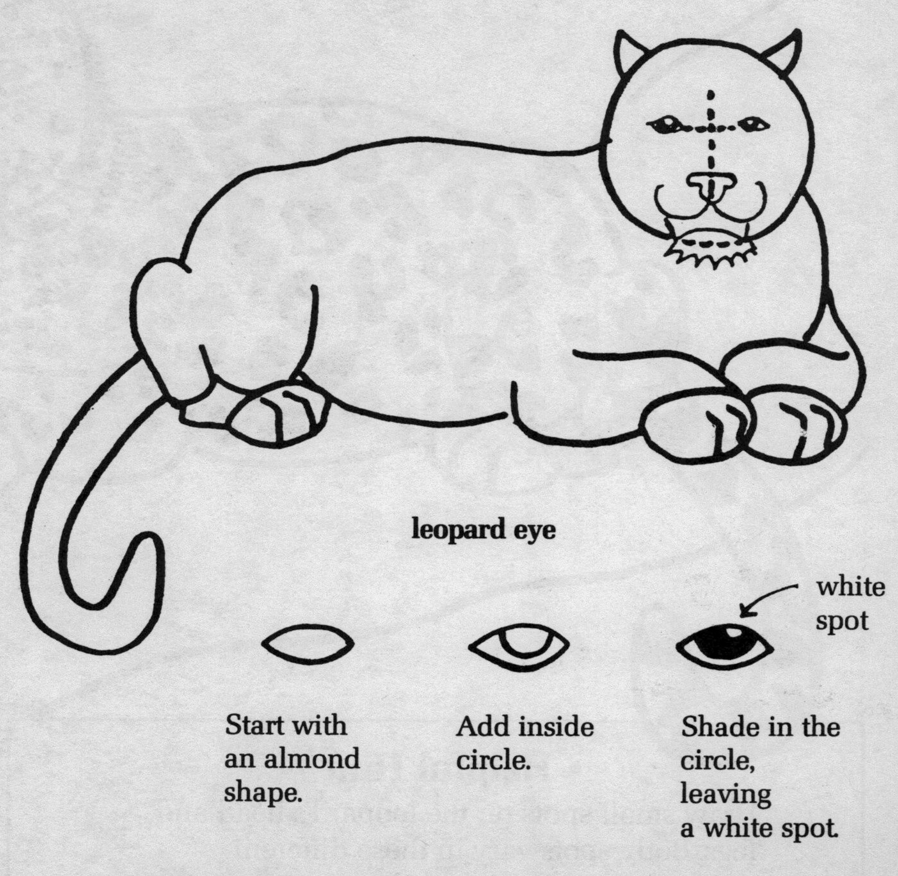

Step 2

Add outlines to connect circles and draw lines to connect the feet circles to the body. These will be the leopard's legs. Draw a cross in head circle, add ears, and draw a tail in the shape of a candy cane. Erase where the dotted lines indicate.

Step 3

Draw eyes left and right of cross intersection. Position the nose at the bottom of cross. Add mouth, chin, and cheeks, and draw lines on feet for the leopard's paws.

Step 4

If you want to show your leopard resting on a tree limb, add lines as shown. Put in whiskers and short hair-line strokes on face, neck, and ears. Draw the leopard's spots (see helpful hint).

• Helpful Hint •

Draw small spots on the leopard's head and legs. Body spots vary in these different patterns!

C shapes, forward and backward

Y shape

O shape

solid spots

Hippopotamus

The hippopotamus is very dependent on water and spends a lot of time in it. Although some of its food is obtained in the water, it likes to eat land grasses best.

Step 1

Start to draw a hippopotamus with the basic body shape, a large cylinder. The legs are smaller cylinder shapes.

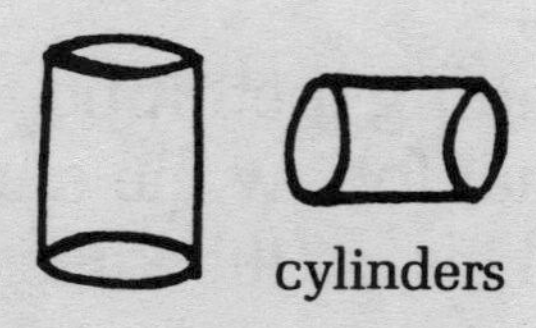

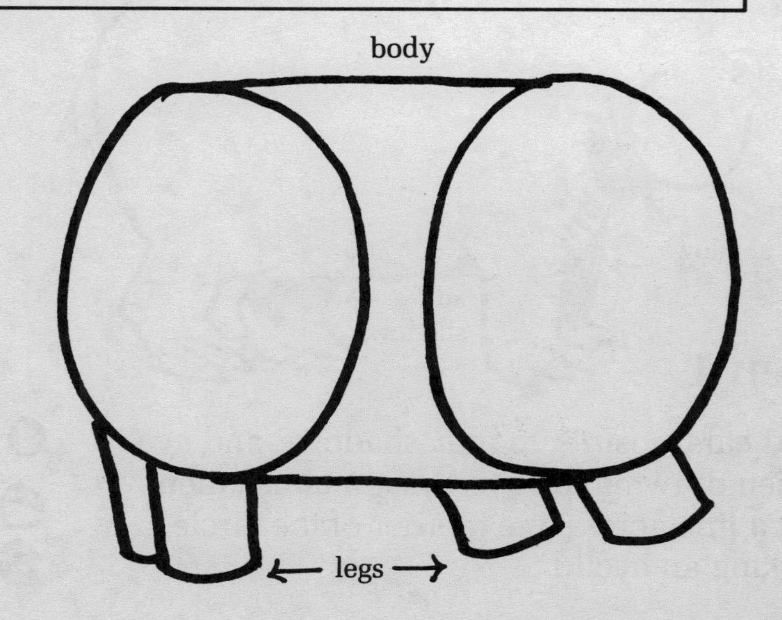

Step 2

Three circles positioned as shown form the basis of the face. Draw feet and toes on the legs. Erase where the dotted lines indicate. Add the tail.

Step 3

Connect the three circles and erase where the dotted lines indicate.

Step 4

Add ears, nostrils, mouth, shadows, and eye. When drawing the eye, draw a circle, then put a line across one quarter of the circle, making an eyelid.

circle

eye lid

eye

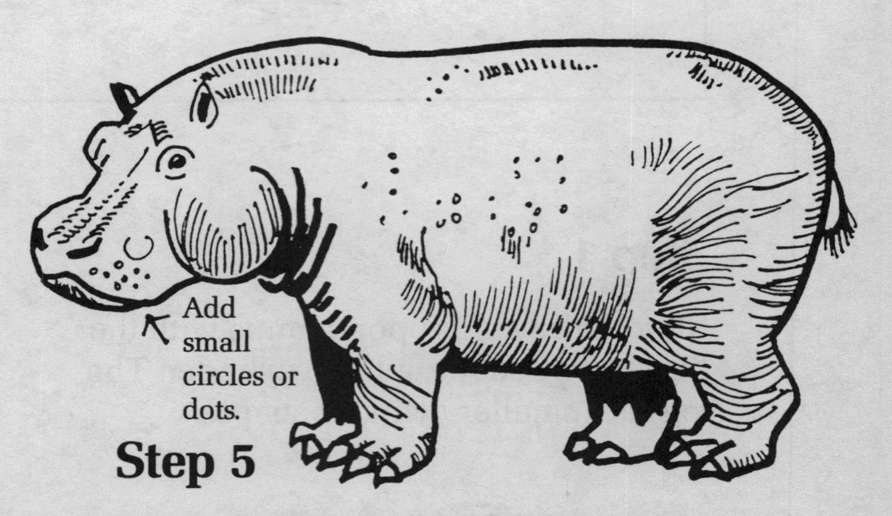

Step 5

When shading the hippo, use various sizes of lines that follow the curves of the body. The wrinkles on the knees curve around the leg. Draw short lines on the face.

Polar Bear

The largest bear in the world, the polar bear lives in the Arctic. Polar bears are excellent swimmers and often build deep snow dens for homes.

Step 1

Start with four circles positioned as shown to draw a polar bear. Put a cylinder shape on the small circle, which will be the bear's head.

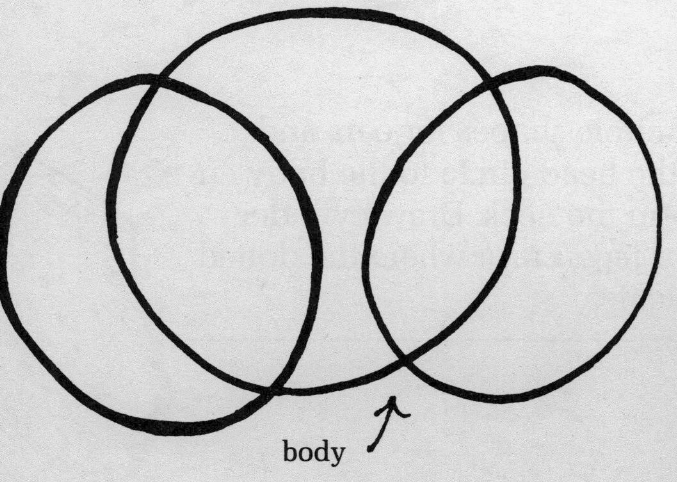

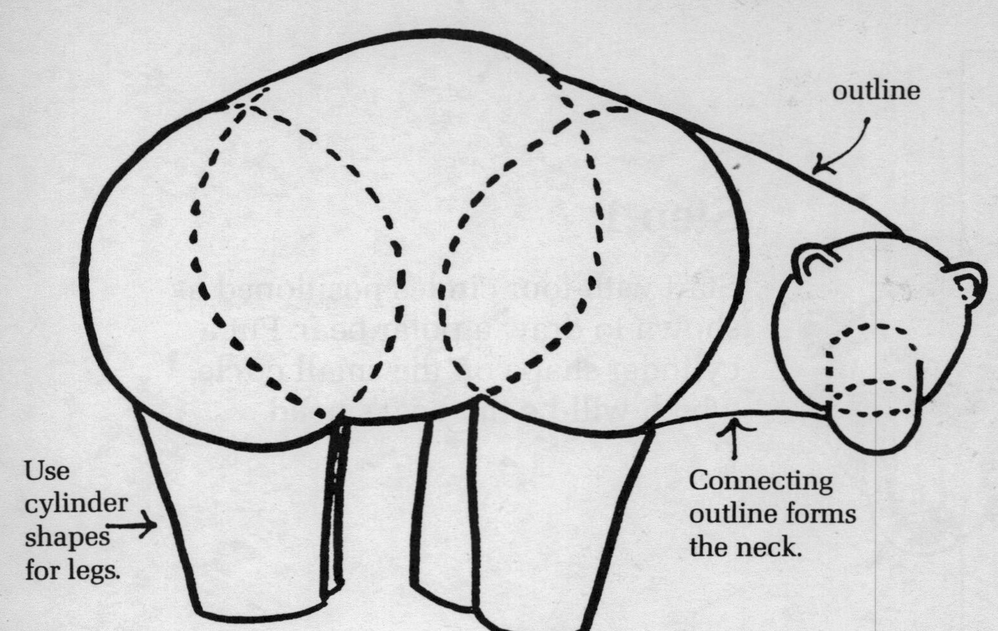

Step 2

Add half-circle shapes for ears and connect the head circle to the body circles to form the neck. Draw cylinder shapes for legs. Erase where the dotted lines indicate.

Step 3

Draw almond-shaped eyes, the nose, and shade in the ears. Draw feet and add the rump.

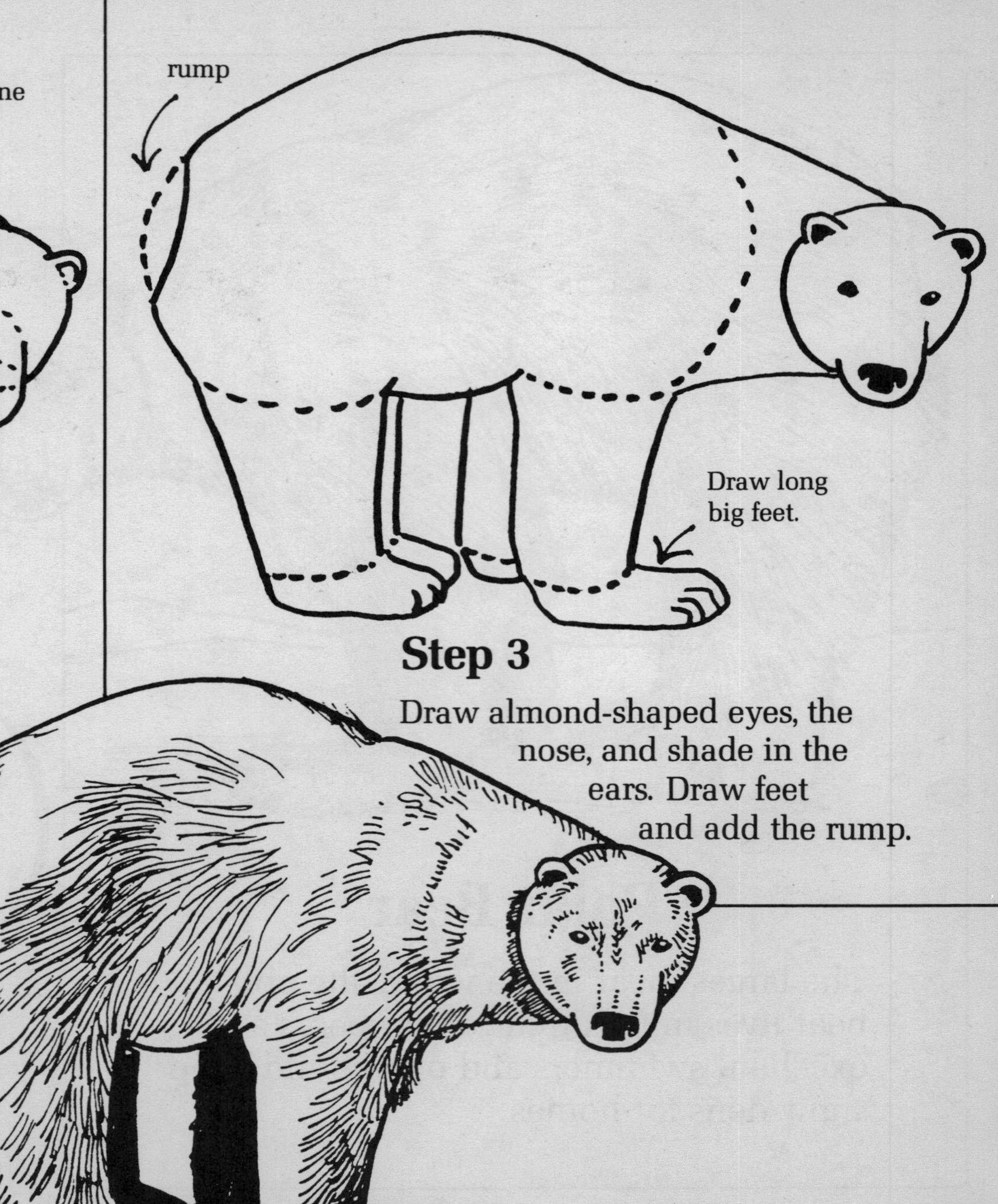

Step 4

Color shadow areas solid. Draw hair lines. Use short hair lines on face, longer lines for body.

Rocky Mountain Goat

This white, long-haired goat is native to the Rocky Mountains. It can climb easily on snow-covered, rocky cliffs.

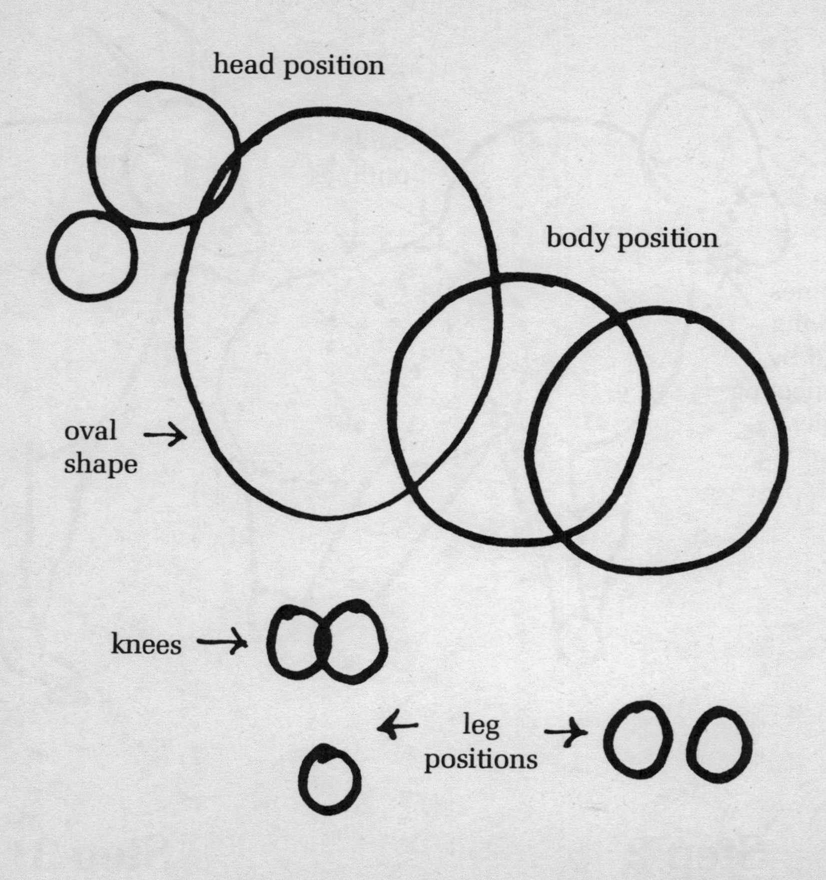

Step 1

Start your Rocky Mountain goat drawing with circles and ovals positioned as shown.

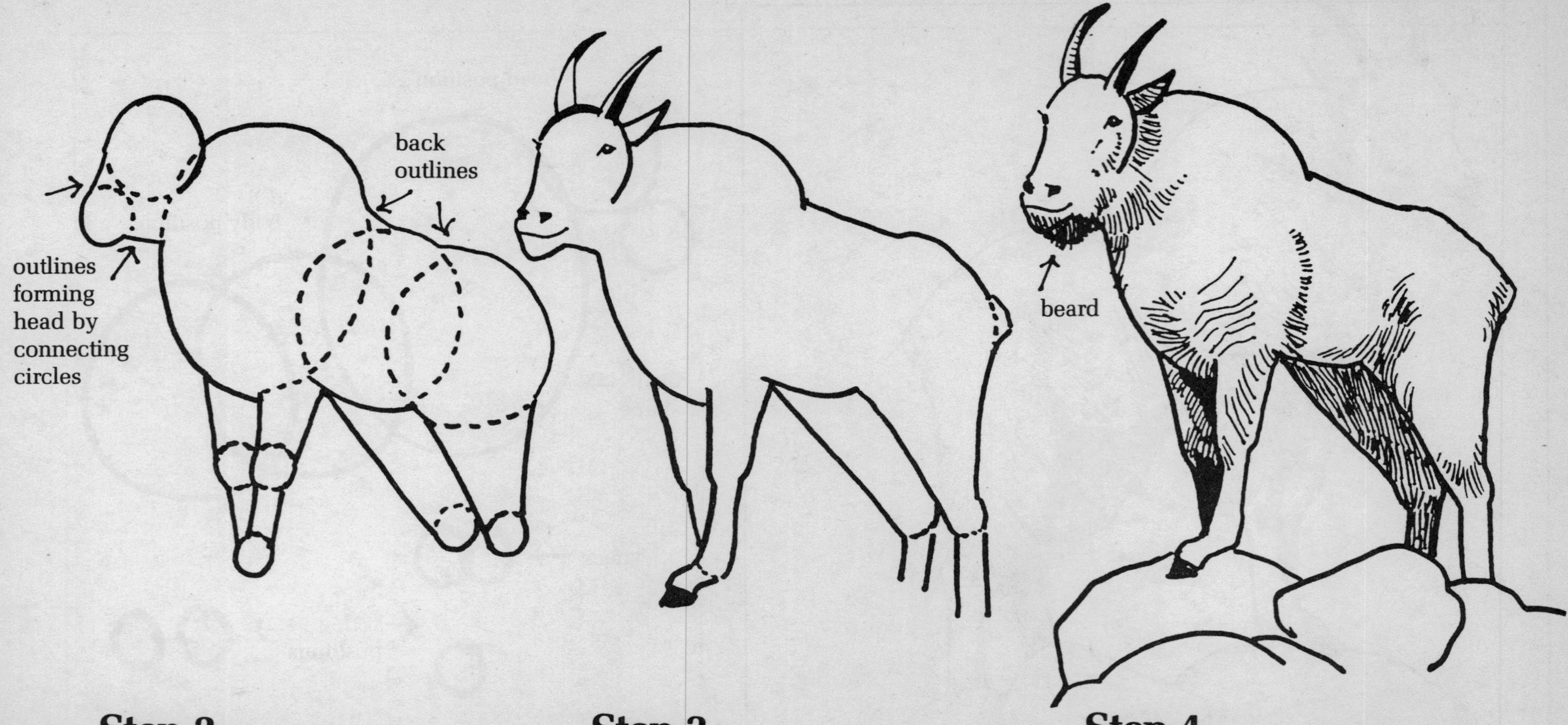

Step 2

Draw lines to connect the circles forming head and back (see arrows). For the front legs, continue the line below the knee to the other circle, forming the lower leg. Erase where the dotted lines indicate.

Step 3

Draw horns, ears, eyes, nostrils, and mouth. Add a hoof to the lower leg and draw a short stubby tail. Draw lower back legs (rocks will hide the hooves). Erase where dotted lines indicate.

Step 4

Add rocks and shadows. Using medium, downward strokes, shade in hair lines. Be sure to add the goat's beard.

Alligator

Alligators spend most of their time basking on river banks. They eat fish, frogs, snakes, and small mammals, and can live for 56 years!

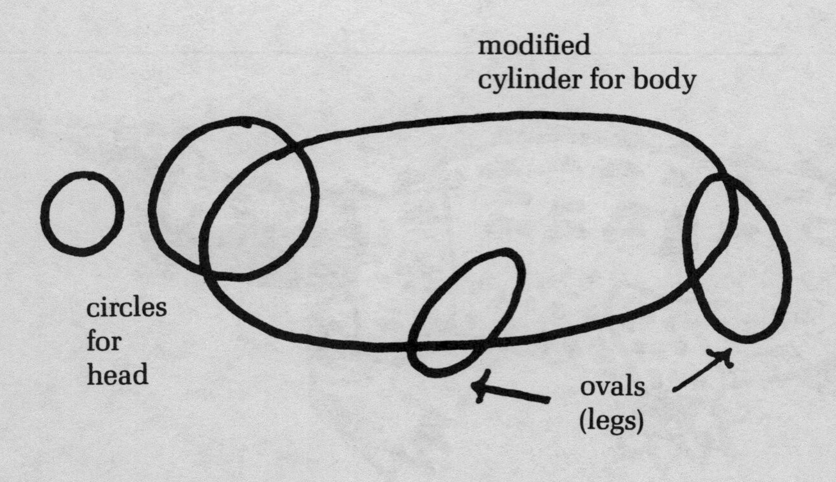

Step 1

Circle, oval, and cylinder shapes positioned as shown are the start of your alligator drawing.

For my body, draw a modified cylinder, a shape similar to a cylinder but not a perfect one.

Step 2

Connect the head circles and add a tail to the end of the cylinder. Draw legs and feet. Erase where the dotted lines indicate.

Step 3

Draw nostrils, a mouth, and an eye, adding a "lump" shape on the head to indicate the alligator's other eye. The eyeball is not visible from this view. Erase where the dotted lines indicate.

Step 4

Draw shadows on the tail and on the legs. For the lumpy skin, draw triangle shapes colored black.

Anteater

The anteater has long, sharp claws with which he digs his food, chiefly ants and termites, from the ground. He then eats them with his pencillike, sticky tongue. Anteaters walk with their claws bent backward.

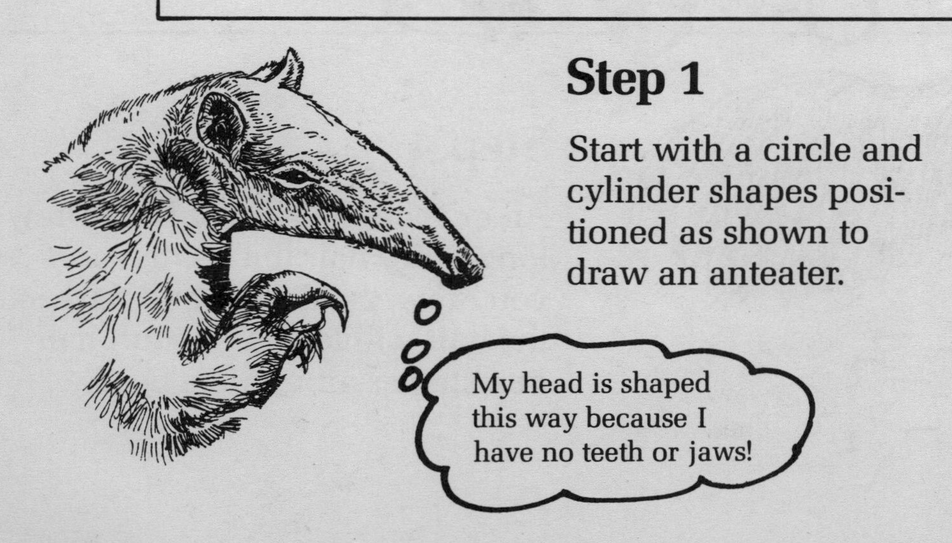

Step 1

Start with a circle and cylinder shapes positioned as shown to draw an anteater.

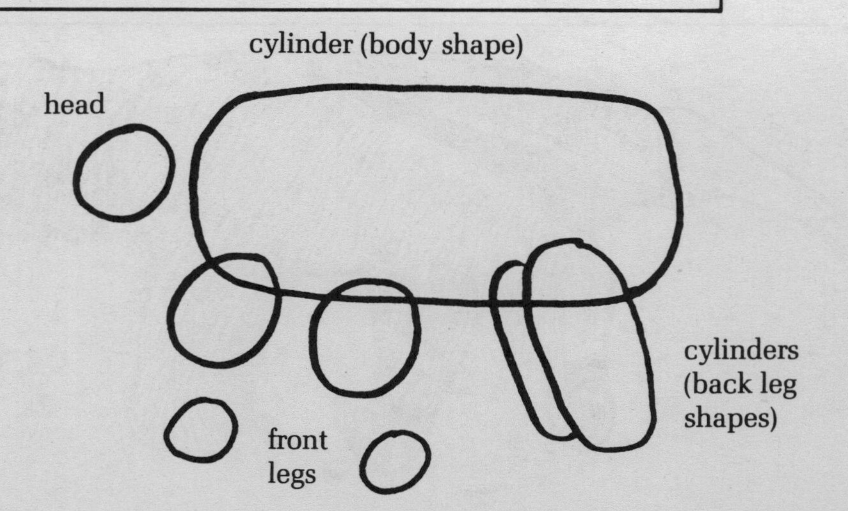

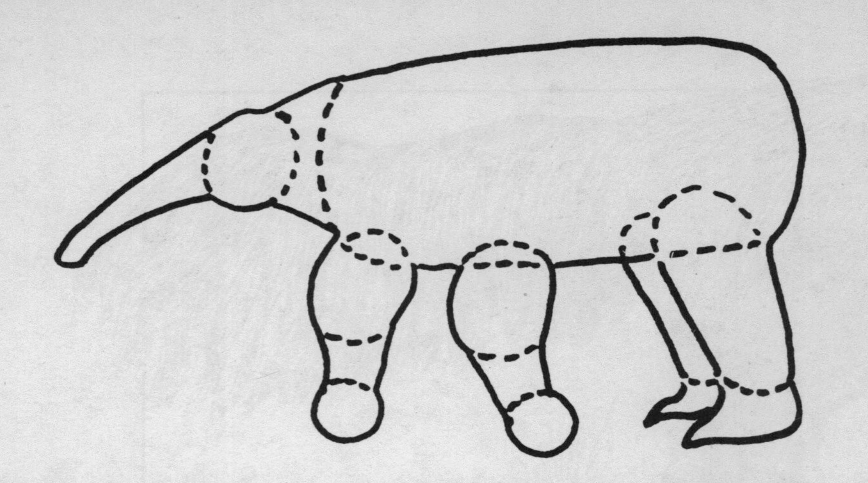

Step 2

Draw lines to connect the head with the body and pencil in the long nose, bending it down slightly. Connect the circles to the body, forming the front legs and draw feet on the back legs. Erase where indicated.

Step 3

Now add the anteater's tiny eye, the ear, and the toes (similar to a triangle shape). For the tail, draw a long, squiggly line. Shade in shadows and markings.

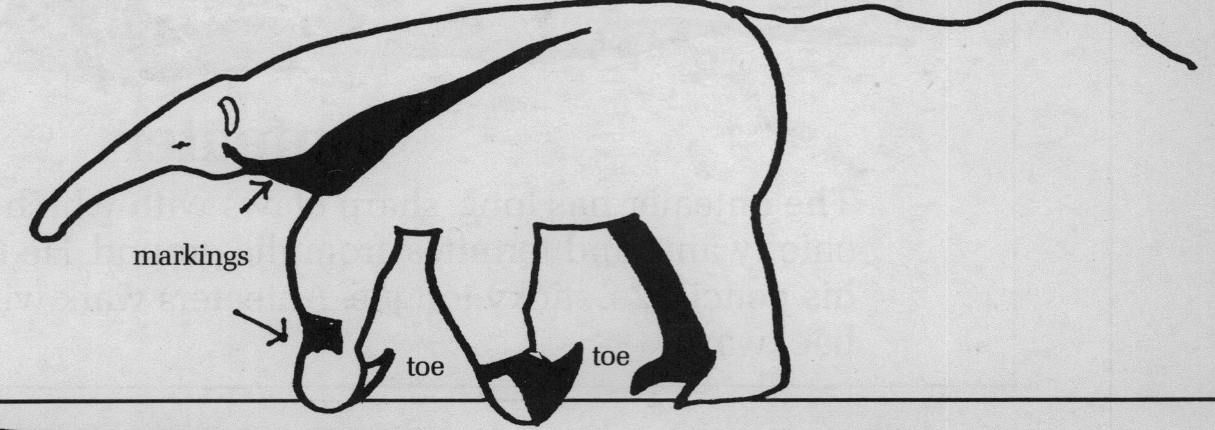

Step 4

An anteater has lots of hair! Draw long, wavy hair lines—the more you draw, the thicker and darker the hair will look. Use short hair-line strokes around the head.

wavy lines

Ostrich

The ostrich, the largest bird in the world, is found in Africa. It is flightless, with long legs and neck and stands eight feet tall!

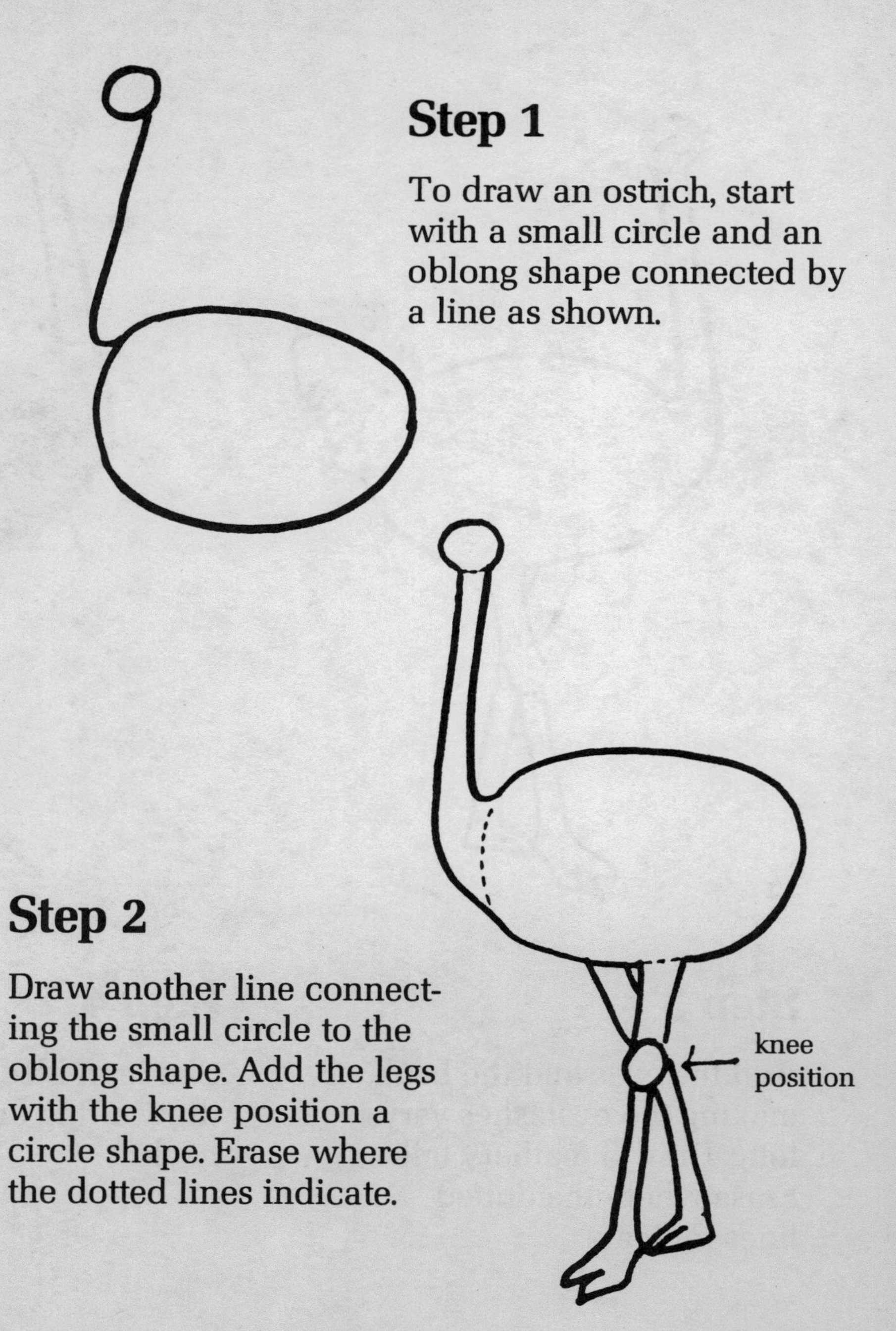

Step 1

To draw an ostrich, start with a small circle and an oblong shape connected by a line as shown.

Step 2

Draw another line connecting the small circle to the oblong shape. Add the legs with the knee position a circle shape. Erase where the dotted lines indicate.

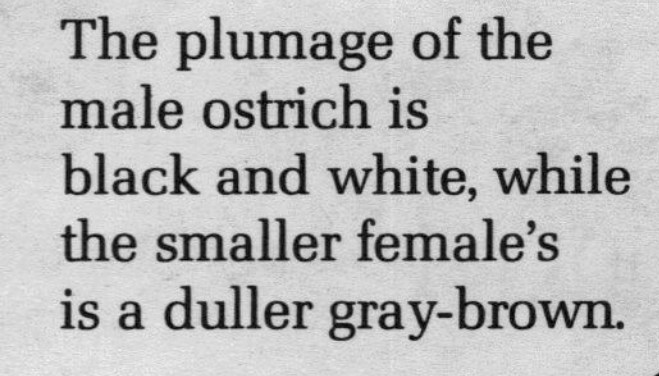

Step 3

Add the eyes and the beak, making the eyelashes very long. Draw a feathery tail. Erase where the dotted lines indicate.

Step 4

Shade in black areas and draw a ring around the neck.

Wild Boar

The upper canine teeth of the wild boar can be fatal to smaller animals that bother him. Usually, though, it eats insects, mushrooms, roots, and fruits.

Step 1

Start to draw a wild boar by making a cone, oval, and circle as shown. Then put a small oval at the end of the cone.

cone

oval

circle

small oval at end of cone

Step 2

Erase where the dotted lines indicate and draw circles for the knee positions. Add hooves.

W shape becomes hoof.

Step 3

Draw lines that connect the body to the knees and hooves. Erase where dotted lines indicate and add ears, eyes, mouth, and tusk. Color in the nose, leaving nostrils white.

Step 4

Draw shadows and add hair lines, making hair appear darker on the nose and around the eyes.

Iguana

Iguanas eat a variety of plant foods, and some larger types may even eat small mammals. They have crests on their heads and backs shaped like the teeth on a comb.

Step 1

Oval and cylinder shapes, positioned as shown, are the start of an iguana. Notice how some oval shapes are placed almost horizontally.

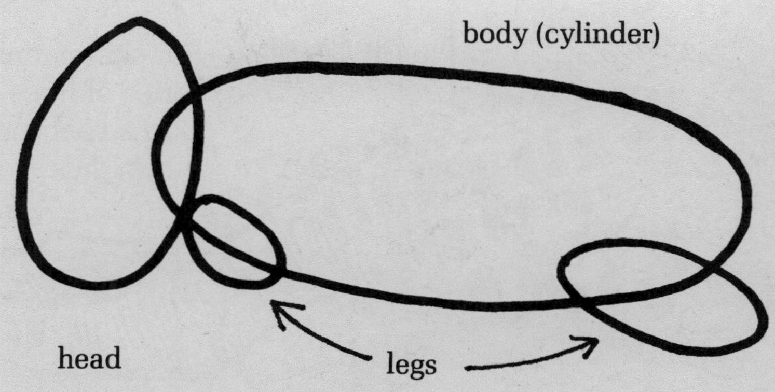

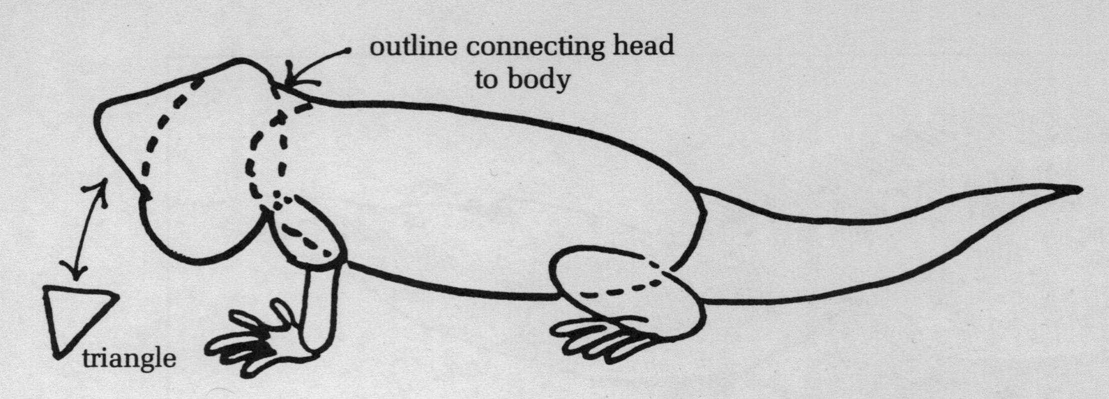

Step 2

Add a triangle shape to the head to form the nose and connect the head to the body (see arrow). Draw the tail and the feet. Erase the dotted lines where indicated.

Step 3

Draw nostril, mouth, chin line, and eye, adding a lump shape by the eye. Like the alligator's eye, it is not visible from this view. Draw the ridge along the head and back.

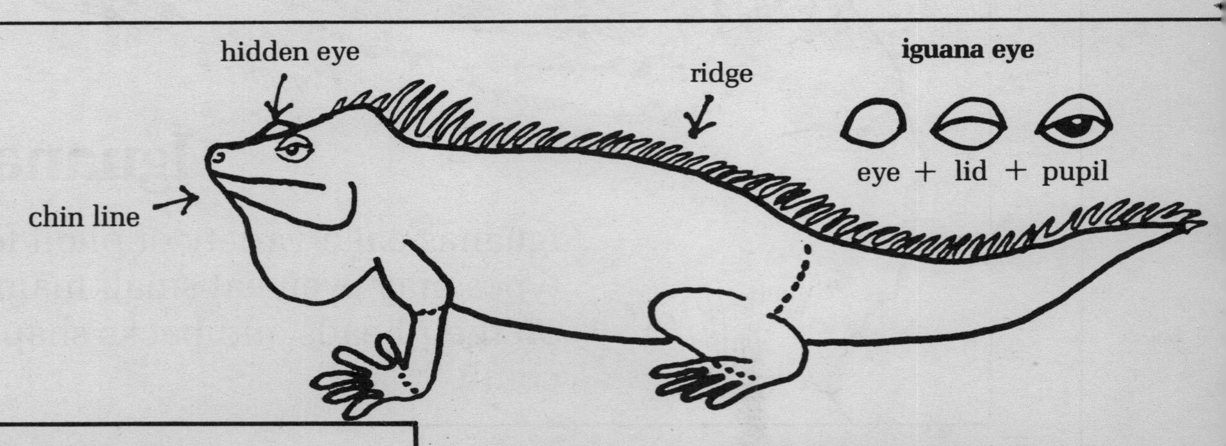

• Helpful Hint •

For skin pattern, draw a series of lines side by side, skip a space, then draw more lines.

Step 4

The iguana is a reptile and does not have hair. To shade its skin pattern, use a series of dots around the face and legs. Draw even lines that form square patterns on body (see example).

You may wish to place your iguana on a rock like this.